101
CHRISTMAS
ORNAMENTS

It's beginning to look a lot like Christmas — especially when you trim the tree with the inventive crafts in 101 Christmas Ornaments! But why stop with the tree? Use your imagination…you can add interest to a window, dress up gift packages, create festive tabletop or mantel displays, and much more. We've included decorations to appeal to every taste and style, from down-home country to gleaming elegance to just plain fun! And for our thrifty recyclers, there's even a collection of ornaments crafted using "trash-can" items such as empty soda bottles and cans, burned-out light bulbs, and empty paper towel tubes. You'll discover lots of projects that make great gifts in themselves — a tiny chalkboard bearing a merry message for teacher, easy-to-assemble snow angels, and a variety of photo ornaments. Turn the page and let the clever crafters at Leisure Arts show you how!

Anne Childs

LEISURE ARTS, INC.
Little Rock, Arkansas

101 CHRISTMAS ORNAMENTS

EDITORIAL STAFF

Vice President and Editor-in-Chief: Anne Van Wagner Childs
Executive Director: Sandra Graham Case
Design Director: Patricia Wallenfang Sowers
Editorial Director: Susan Frantz Wiles
Publications Director: Kristine Anderson Mertes
Creative Art Director: Gloria Bearden

DESIGN

Senior Designers: Cherece Athy Cooper, Cyndi Hansen, and Linda Diehl Tiano
Designers: Polly Tullis Browning, Diana Sanders Cates, Dani Martin, Sandra Spotts Ritchie, Billie Steward, and Anne Pulliam Stocks
Executive Assistant: Debra Smith
Design Assistant: Dani Martin

TECHNICAL

Managing Editor: Sherry Solida Ford
Senior Technical Writer: K. J. Smith
Technical Writers: Leslie Schick Gorrell, Jennifer Potts Hutchings, and Theresa Hicks Young
Copy Editor: Susan Frazier
Technical Associate: Candice Treat Murphy
Technical Assistant: Sharon Gillam

EDITORIAL

Managing Editor: Linda L. Trimble
Senior Associate Editor: Shelby D. Brewer
Associate Editors: Darla Burdette Kelsay, Suzie Puckett, and Hope Turner
Copy Editor: Susan McManus Johnson

ART

Book/Magazine Graphic Art Director: Diane Thomas
Graphic Artist and Color Technician: Mark Hawkins
Photography Stylists: Ellen J. Clifton, Tiffany Huffman, Elizabeth Lackey, and Janna Laughlin
Staff Photographer: Russell Ganser
Publishing Systems Administrator: Becky Riddle
Publishing Systems Assistants: Myra S. Means and Chris Wertenberger

PROMOTIONS

Managing Editor: Alan Caudle
Associate Editor: Steven M. Cooper
Designer: Dale Rowett
Art Operations Director: Jeff Curtis
Graphic Artist: Deborah Kelly

BUSINESS STAFF

Publisher: Rick Barton
Vice President, Finance: Tom Siebenmorgen
Director of Corporate Planning and Development: Laticia Mull Cornett
Vice President, Retail Marketing: Bob Humphrey
Vice President, National Accounts: Pam Stebbins

Retail Marketing Director: Margaret Sweetin
General Merchandise Manager: Cathy Laird
Vice President, Operations: Jim Dittrich
Distribution Director: Rob Thieme
Retail Customer Service Manager: Wanda Price
Print Production Manager: Fred F. Pruss

International Standard Book Number 1-57486-173-5

10 9 8 7 6 5 4 3

Table of Contents

Table of Contents

TRASH TO TREASURE 56

Table of Contents

A TOUCH OF ELEGANCE 78

COUNTRY CHRISTMAS

If you enjoy the warmth of a country Christmas, you'll love these cozy trims! Pull out your scrap basket to make homey pieced ornaments, or grab an embroidery needle and whip up some simple cross-stitched designs. Do you collect buttons? Show them off on our easy-to-make angels or use them to dress up a frosty friend! If you prefer the natural look, craft rustic pomander balls or a woodland Santa with a birch-bark hat…stitch up a flock of redbirds to brighten the tree…or paint a pair of trout for a favorite angler. Get set for a down-home holiday!

Make your Christmas tree a haven for the birds! These cheery cardinals can be made in a snap using red felt and a hot glue gun. But don't forget their houses! Fashioned from toilet paper tubes and tree bark, the rustic dwellings make pleasant perches for your feathered friends, as well as nice additions to your evergreen.

CHRISTMAS CARDINALS

For each ornament, you will need tracing paper, red felt, black embroidery floss, orange and black acrylic paint, small paintbrush, hot glue gun, and a 9" length of clear nylon thread.

1. Trace patterns, page 106, onto tracing paper. Using patterns, cut two bodies and two wings from felt.

2. Matching edges, place each pair of shapes together. Using six strands of floss, work Overcast Stitch, page 126, around edges.

3. Paint an orange beak and a black mask on cardinal; allow to dry. Glue wing in place.

4. For hanger, knot ends of thread together; glue knot to back of ornament.

RUSTIC BIRDHOUSES

For each ornament, you will need a craft knife; toilet tissue tube; crackling medium; white, antique white, red, and brown acrylic paint; foam brushes; twigs; corrugated craft cardboard; clear nylon thread; toothbrush; lightweight cardboard; hot glue gun; tree bark; miniature artificial greenery with pinecones; and a small artificial cardinal.

Refer to Painting Basics, page 124, before beginning project. Allow paint and crackling medium to dry after each application.

1. Use craft knife to cut tube to desired length; cut a 3/8" dia. hole in tube.

2. Following crackling medium manufacturer's instructions and using brown for basecoat and antique white for top coat, paint tube.

3. Use a pencil to punch a small hole in tube 1/4" below larger hole. Glue a 1" long twig into small hole.

4. For roof, cut a 2" x 4" rectangle from corrugated cardboard. Matching short edges, fold cardboard in half; unfold.

5. Dry brush roof with red paint; spatter with white paint.

6. For hanger, take a small stitch through top of roof with a 9" length of thread; knot ends together.

7. For roof brace, cut a 1" x 4" strip from lightweight cardboard. Fold strip at center and 1" from center on each side (Fig. 1). Glue ends of brace inside top of tube; glue roof to top of brace.

Fig. 1

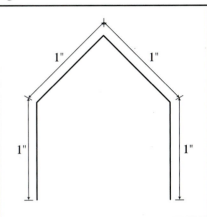

8. For brace at bottom of tube, draw around tube on lightweight cardboard. Cut out circle inside drawn line; glue inside bottom of tube. Glue birdhouse to bark.

9. Dry brush greenery and pinecones with white paint; glue to roof. Glue cardinal to bark.

Our homespun Santa and snowman ornaments are perfect for adding a touch of country charm to your holiday decor. Reminding us of quaint and cozy Christmases past, the homey adornments are sure to be cherished for years to come!

HOMESPUN ORNAMENTS

You will need paper-backed fusible web; scraps of assorted fabrics, ecru felt, cotton batting, and muslin; assorted colors of embroidery floss; pink colored pencil; black permanent fine-point marker; pinking shears; assorted buttons; and jute twine.

Refer to Making Appliqués, page 124, and Embroidery Stitches, page 125, before beginning project. Use two strands of floss for all embroidery.

Santa Ornament

1. For Santa ornament, use patterns, page 102, to make coat, hat, and two mitten appliqués from fabrics. Make beard, mustache, hat trim, pom-pom, and two cuff appliqués from felt.

2. Cut two 5" squares from fabric, one 5" square from batting, and one 4½" square from muslin. Press edges of muslin square ¼" to wrong side. Arrange appliqués on muslin and fuse in place. Use pencil to color cheeks and marker to draw eyes.

3. Work Blanket Stitch along edges of hat and coat. Work Running Stitch along center of each cuff and along edges of each remaining felt piece.

4. Use pencil to lightly write "HO HO HO" on muslin. Work Running Stitch over drawn lines.

5. Center appliquéd muslin piece on one fabric square; use Running Stitch to stitch in place. Sew a button to each corner of muslin.

6. Matching edges, layer batting square between fabric squares. For hanger, tie a small bow in center of a 10" length of jute; pin jute ends between layers at top of ornament. Work Running Stitch ½" from edge to sew layers together. Use pinking shears to trim ¼" from each edge.

Snowman Ornament

1. For snowman ornament, use patterns, page 102, to make hat and scarf appliqués from fabrics. Make snowman appliqué from felt.

2. Cut two 5" x 6" rectangles from fabric, one 5" x 6" rectangle from batting, and one 4½" x 5½" rectangle from muslin. Press edges of muslin rectangle ¼" to wrong side. Arrange appliqués on muslin and fuse in place. Cut a ¼" x 2" strip of fabric for scarf; knot in center and tack to one end of scarf.

3. Work Blanket Stitch along edges of snowman. Work Running Stitch for arms and along edges of hat.

4. Use Straight Stitch to work snowflakes, Running Stitch for mouth, French Knots for eyes, and Satin Stitch for nose. Sew three small buttons to snowman front.

5. Refer to Steps 5 and 6 of Santa Ornament to complete snowman ornament.

FABRIC FANCIES

*S*ave your fabric scraps to make these fun tree trimmers! Hide a gift of cash or candy in the clever buttoned-up star, or craft a peaceful dove to perch among the evergreen boughs.

SURPRISE GIFT ORNAMENT

You will need 8" squares of paper-backed fusible web, red and green fabrics; tracing paper; red thread; pinking shears; small, tissue-wrapped gift; ⁵⁄₈" dia. red button; and an 18" length of ⁷⁄₈"w red wired ribbon.

1. Use web to fuse wrong sides of fabric pieces together.

2. Trace star pattern, page 101, onto tracing paper; cut out. Draw around pattern on fused fabric. Using red thread, machine stitch along drawn line. Using pinking shears, cut out star ¼" outside stitching line.

3. Bring star tips together at center of star, enclosing gift; hand sew tips together. Sew button over star tips.

4. For hanger, gather and stitch center of ribbon length to top of ornament; leaving a loop for hanging, tie ribbon ends into a bow.

APPLIQUÉ DOVE

You will need paper-backed fusible web, scraps of assorted fabrics and batting, clear nylon thread, red and black embroidery floss, pinking shears, large needle, and an 18" length of ¹⁄₈"w satin ribbon.

1. Using patterns, page 111, follow *Making Appliqués*, page 124, to make body, wing, beak, leaf, and stem appliqués, and eight berry appliqués from fabrics.

2. Cut two 7" squares from fabric for background and one 7" square from batting. On one fabric square, arrange appliqués, overlapping as necessary, and fuse in place. Use nylon thread and a narrow zigzag stitch to machine stitch along all raw edges of appliqués.

3. Using three strands of black floss, work a French Knot, page 125, for eye on dove.

4. Matching edges, layer batting square between wrong sides of fabric squares. Using three strands of red floss, work a Running Stitch, page 126, ¼" from outer edges of fused motif. Use pinking shears to cut out ornament ¼" outside stitching.

5. For hanger, use needle to thread ribbon through top edge of ornament. Knot ribbon, leaving a loop for hanging; tie ends into a bow.

CHRISTMAS CATCH

*R*eel in the Christmas spirit
with this festive catch! Just paint
wooden fish ornaments and hang
them on the tree. What a great way
to "lure" holiday smiles!

CATCH OF THE DAY
You will need an unfinished wooden fish
ornament (our ornament has two
1⁷⁄₈" x 5" fish linked with chain); white,
gold, red, green, dark green, and black
acrylic paint; paintbrushes; and a natural
sponge piece.

Refer to Painting Basics, page 124,
before beginning project. Allow paint to
dry after each application.

1. Paint tail and top one-third of each fish
green; paint remainder of fish gold.

2. Sponge Paint over green with dark
green. Use red to Sponge Paint bottom
edge of fish, over line between green and
gold areas, and on tail.

3. Use black paint thinned with water to
paint gills and detail lines on tail and fins.
Highlight gills with white paint thinned
with water.

4. Paint a white dot for each eye, then a
smaller black dot for pupil.

THE HEART OF CHRISTMAS

Everyone knows that the heart of Christmas is love — gatherings with loved ones bring out the best of the season. Capture those sentiments with this padded, bow-tied ornament.

PADDED HEART

You will need paper-backed fusible web, 5" square of fabric, pinking shears, 6" x 6½" piece of green felt, red and green embroidery floss, assorted buttons, two 7" x 8" pieces of red felt, polyester fiberfill, and ³⁄₈"w green satin ribbon.

1. Using patterns, page 115, follow *Making Appliqués*, page 124, to make one small heart appliqué from fabric and one medium heart appliqué (cut out with pinking shears) from green felt.

2. Fuse fabric heart to felt heart. Referring to *Embroidery Stitches*, pages 125, and using three strands of floss, work red Running Stitch along edge of fabric heart. Use green floss to sew on buttons, to work French Knots around buttons, and to work Stem Stitch for stems.

3. Center green heart on one red felt piece and fuse in place. Layer red felt pieces and use pinking shears to cut ½" outside green heart.

4. Using green floss and leaving an opening for stuffing, use Overcast Stitch to sew hearts together. Stuff ornament with fiberfill; sew opening closed.

5. For hanger, tie ends of a 16" length of ribbon into a bow, leaving a 4" loop; stitch bow to top of heart.

SCHOOL DAYS

Bedazzle your child's favorite teacher with this school days ornament! A square of black poster board forms the "chalkboard." Frame it with painted craft sticks and use colored pencils to add a merry message.

MERRY MESSAGE FOR TEACHER

You will need tracing paper; stylus; transfer paper; 4" square of black poster board; white, red, and green colored pencils; six ¼" x 5½" craft sticks; utility scissors; hot glue gun; two 1" long plastic candy canes; 6" length of ⅛"w satin ribbon; clear nylon thread; and a 1" dia. gold bell.

1. Trace pattern, page 116, onto tracing paper. Use stylus and transfer paper to transfer design to poster board. Use pencils to color design.

2. For sides of frame, use utility scissors to cut ⅝" off each end of two craft sticks. Glue one trimmed craft stick to each side edge of poster board. For top and bottom of frame, glue craft sticks across ends of trimmed craft sticks. Glue remaining craft sticks diagonally across top of frame, with ends overlapping.

3. Glue candy canes to ornament. Tie ribbon into a bow; glue to top of ornament.

4. Thread a 9" length of nylon thread through top of bell; knot ends. Glue ends to top back ornament.

COZY COUNTRY CHRISTMAS

You can have a down-home country Christmas even if you live in the big city! Our folksy stocking trims are a cinch to make: just glue together the felt shapes and make a few stitches along the edges. Hang the stocking ornaments on a twig tree, and for a homey finishing touch, adorn the branches with jute garland embellished with buttons and flannel scraps.

FELT STOCKING ORNAMENTS

You will need assorted scraps of felt and flannel, pinking shears, tracing paper, fabric glue, black embroidery floss, hot glue gun, assorted small buttons, and jute twine.

1. Cut four 4" squares from felt and four 3¼" squares from flannel. Using pinking shears, cut four 5" squares from felt.

2. Trace patterns, page 104, onto tracing paper. Using patterns, cut four stockings, four cuffs, three stars, and one of each additional shape from felt.

3. Referring to photo, layer pieces together to make four ornaments; use dots of fabric glue to secure and allow to dry. Following *Embroidery Stitches*, page 125, and using three strands of floss, work Running Stitch or Blanket Stitch along edge of each shape; work French Knots and Cross Stitches inside shapes.

4. Hot glue buttons to corners of ornaments.

5. For each hanger, knot ends of a 9" length of twine together to form a loop; hot glue knot to back of ornament.

COUNTRIFIED GARLAND

You will need a 6' length of heavy jute twine, hot glue gun, assorted buttons,

pinking shears, and assorted flannel scraps.

1. Knot each end of twine.

2. Spacing randomly, glue buttons to twine.

3. Use pinking shears to cut ½" x 4" strips from flannel scraps. Knot strips to twine between buttons.

JAUNTY SNOWMAN

This little snowman will charm everyone with his friendly smile! Tiny painted flowerpots form his sturdy legs and jaunty hat.

FESTIVE SNOWMAN

You will need a 6" length of 19-gauge black wire; 1³/₄" dia. clay flowerpot; 1¹/₂" dia. and 2¹/₂" dia. wooden balls; two 1¹/₄" dia. clay flowerpots; white, orange, and black acrylic paint; paintbrushes; toothbrush; ¹/₂" long twig for nose; hot glue gun; two 1¹/₂" long twigs for arms; and a scrap of fabric.

Refer to Painting Basics, page 124, before beginning project. Allow paint to dry after each application.

1. For hanger, fold wire length in half; twist ends together. Insert ends through hole in bottom of large pot; bend to keep in place.

2. Paint balls white and pots black. Lightly Spatter Paint large pot with white paint. Paint ¹/₂" long twig orange.

3. Glue balls together. Glue large pot in place for hat; glue small pots in place for legs. Glue arms to large ball; glue nose to face.

4. Paint white snowflake on hat, black eyes and mouth on face, and black buttons on body.

5. For hat trim, cut a ¹/₄"w strip from fabric to fit around hat; glue in place. For muffler, cut a ¹/₂" x 10" strip from fabric; fringe ends and tie around neck.

*B*ring the beauty of the outdoors indoors with these simple yet elegant ornaments! Our nature-inspired pomanders are as easy to make as they are pretty: simply cover papier-mâché balls with dried beans, berries, and seeds for a naturally charming way to trim your tree!

NATURAL ORNAMENTS

For each ornament, you will need a 2¹/₂" dia. papier-mâché ball, craft glue, hot glue gun, 5" length of 19-gauge craft wire, one large artificial cranberry, and clear acrylic spray sealer.

For leafy ornament, you will also need red acrylic paint, paintbrush, tracing paper, green handmade paper, straight pins, and dried canella berries.

For flowery ornament, you will also need yellow ochre acrylic paint, paintbrush, split peas, rye flakes, mustard seeds, pumpkin seeds, and adzuki beans.

For wheat seeds ornament, you will also need soybeans, adzuki beans, pumpkin seeds, mustard seeds, and soft white wheat seeds.

Use hot glue for all gluing unless otherwise indicated. Allow paint, craft glue, and sealer to dry after each application.

1. For each hanger, insert one end of wire 1" into ball; glue to secure. Place cranberry on wire; bend wire to form hanger.

2. For leafy ornament, paint ball red; allow to dry.

3. Trace leaf pattern, page 116, onto tracing paper. Using pattern, cut 26 leaves from handmade paper. Referring to Fig. 1, fold each leaf to form crease.

Fig. 1

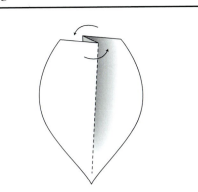

4. Using craft glue, glue rows of leaves to upper half of ball; allow to dry. Inserting a pin through each berry, pin berries to ball. Glue additional berries around hanger below cranberry.

5. For flowery ornament, paint ball yellow ochre.

6. Glue rows of split peas to bottom half of ball, dividing area into four sections (Fig. 2). Using craft glue, glue rye flakes on ball to cover each section.

Fig. 2

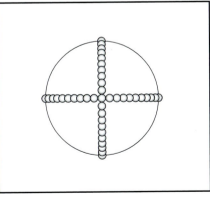

7. Glue a ⁵/₈" dia. circle of mustard seeds above each row of peas to form flower center. Glue pumpkin seeds around flower centers for petals. Glue pumpkin seeds around hanger; glue adzuki beans between pumpkin seeds.

8. For wheat seeds ornament, glue a horizontal row of soybeans around center of ball; glue eight rows of soybeans to top half of ball, dividing ball into eight sections (Fig. 3). Glue one adzuki bean and two pumpkin seeds at bottom of each section; fill in remainder of section with mustard seeds. Using craft glue, glue wheat seeds to bottom half of ornament.

Fig. 3

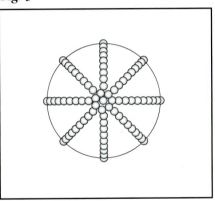

9. Spray each ornament with acrylic sealer.

19

WOODLAND CHARM

*B*ring woodland style to the
holidays with our rustic Santa.
He's super simple to create using a
papier-mâché ball and a birch cone.
Wool roving provides a realistic beard.

WOODLAND SANTA

You will need a 4½" papier-mâché egg;
white, peach, and black acrylic paint;
paintbrushes; hot glue gun; wool roving;
preserved berries, greenery, and
miniature pinecones; 3" x 7" birch cone;
ecru reindeer moss; and a 4" length of
19-gauge wire.

*Allow paint to dry after each
application.*

1. Paint egg peach. Paint eyes and
eyebrows black; paint white highlights in
eyes.

2. Glue wool roving to egg for hair,
mustache, and beard. Glue a berry to face
for nose.

3. For hat, glue cone to head. Glue
greenery, berries, and pinecones to hat.
Glue moss to top of hat.

4. For hanger, bend wire to form a loop;
glue ends to back of ornament.

COUNTRY ANGELS

With their folksy charm and button wings, these angels are sure to bring Christmas joy! Our cheery cherubs are easily crafted using felt and fiberfill. Besides trimming the tree, the angelic adornments are also perfect for dressing up gift packages. What a heavenly idea!

BUTTON ANGELS

For each ornament, you will need tracing paper, felt, embroidery floss, polyester fiberfill, hot glue gun, a 1¼" length of ½"w lace trim, a 6" length of 1/16"w satin ribbon, a 5" length of 19-gauge wire, 25mm wooden bead, jute twine, brown fine-point marker, two large buttons, assorted small buttons, and a 9" length of clear nylon thread.

1. For each angel, trace body pattern, page 112, onto tracing paper. Fold felt in half. Placing dashed line on pattern on fold, pin pattern to felt. Cut shape from felt; keep shape folded.

2. Using embroidery floss, work a Running Stitch, page 126, ¼" from long edges on each side of body, lightly stuffing shape with fiberfill before finishing final seam.

3. For halo, form a ¾" dia. circle in center of wire; twist wire ends together. Glue wire ends into hole in bead.

4. For hair, cut several 4" lengths of twine. Untwist lengths, arrange on head, and glue in place; trim as desired.

5. Using brown marker, draw eyes on bead. Glue bead to top of body.

6. Glue lace along top edge of body for collar. Tie ribbon into a bow and glue to collar.

7. Glue large buttons to back of body for wings. Glue small buttons to front of angel.

8. For hanger, knot ends of nylon thread together; glue knot to back of ornament.

Capture the fun of Christmas with this whimsical ornament! With his spindly arms and legs and fuzzy felt beard, our silly St. Nick is sure to bring plenty of smiles.

HOMEY SANTA

You will need red, green, and black felt; polyester fiberfill; muslin; black embroidery floss; red colored pencil; tracing paper; white plush felt; scraps of assorted red and white print fabrics; tea bag; hot glue gun; and a 3/4" dia. black button.

1. For body, cut two 5 1/2" x 6 1/2" pieces from red felt. Referring to Fig. 1 and using a 1/2" seam allowance, sew pieces together, leaving openings for head, arms, and legs.

Fig. 1

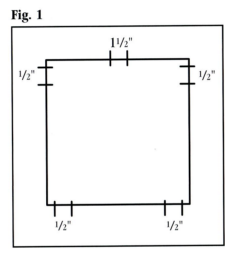

2. Turn body right side out; stuff with fiberfill.

3. Cut two 2 1/2" x 3" pieces of muslin. Use pattern, page 100, and follow *Sewing Shapes*, page 124, to make head.

4. Using three strands of black embroidery floss, work French Knots, page 125, for eyes. Use red pencil to color cheeks.

5. Stuff head with fiberfill. Insert neck 3/4" into body; stitch head to body, stitching opening closed.

6. Trace beard, mustache, mitten, and boot patterns, page 100, onto tracing paper; cut out.

7. Cut two 5 1/2" squares from red felt. Use pattern, page 100, and follow Sewing Shapes to make hat.

8. For hat trim and pom-pom, cut a 1/2" x 5" strip and a 5/8" dia. circle from white felt. Glue hat trim and pom-pom to hat.

9. To tea-dye fabrics, steep tea bag in two cups hot water; allow to cool and remove tea bag. Soak fabrics in tea until desired color is achieved; remove from tea, allow to dry, and press.

10. From fabrics, cut two 1 1/2" x 8" strips for arms and two 1 1/4" x 10" strips for legs. Matching right sides, fold each fabric strip in half lengthwise; use a 1/4" seam allowance to stitch long edges together. Turn right side out and press. Insert one end of each limb 3/4" into openings in body; stitch limbs to body, stitching openings closed. Knot each limb for elbow or knee.

11. Using patterns, cut four mittens from green felt and four boots from black felt. Glue two mittens together over end of each arm; glue two boots together over end of each leg.

12. Using patterns, cut mustache and beard from white felt. Glue top edge of beard, then mustache to face.

13. For suit trim, cut a 1/2" x 6" and a 3/4" x 11 1/2" piece of white felt; glue in place at center front and around lower edge of body.

14. For belt, cut a 3/4" x 10 1/2" strip of black felt. Glue belt in place, overlapping ends at center back; glue button to belt.

BASKETFUL OF CHEER

A tisket, a tasket, a basketful of country Christmas cheer! Filled with greenery, berries, and fragrant cinnamon sticks, this simple accent is perfect for your country kitchen… or make several to share at a holiday ornament exchange.

BERRY BASKET

You will need a hot glue gun, small grapevine star, small basket with handle, green acrylic paint, paintbrush, preserved greenery and berries, cinnamon sticks, and a 22" length of 1"w wired ribbon.

1. Glue star to front of basket. Dry brush basket and star with green paint; allow to dry.

2. Arrange greenery, berries, and cinnamon sticks inside basket and glue in place.

3. Leaving a loop for hanging, tie ribbon into a bow around basket handle.

PEACEFUL MOSAIC

This darling dove ornament promises to bring peaceful tidings to your home! Simply cut out felt appliqués and arrange them to create the dove's shape; then fuse them onto a black background. Add a few embroidery stitches here and there, and your mosaic masterpiece is complete!

FELT MOSAIC DOVE

You will need white, gold, red, green, and black felt; poster board; pinking shears; paper-backed fusible web; tracing paper; white, red, green, and black embroidery floss; and a hot glue gun.

Refer to Embroidery Stitches, page 125, and use three strands of floss for all embroidery.

1. Cut a $4^3/4$" x $5^3/4$" piece from red felt and a $4^1/2$" x $5^1/2$" piece from poster board.

2. Using pinking shears, cut a $4^1/2$" x $5^1/2$" piece from black felt, $5^1/2$" x $6^1/2$" and $1/2$" x 3" pieces from green felt, and a 6" x 7" piece from gold felt.

3. Use patterns, page 104, and follow *Making Appliqués*, page 124, to make twelve leaf appliqués from green felt, four berry appliqués from red felt, one beak appliqué from gold felt, and dove body appliqués from white felt. Arrange appliqués on black felt piece and fuse in place.

4. Trace "Peace" pattern, page 104, onto tracing paper; pin pattern to black felt piece. Using white floss, work Stem Stitch over pattern; remove pattern. Using white floss, work Running Stitch along edges of black felt piece. Work green Straight

Stitches on leaves and red Straight Stitches on berries. Work black French Knot for eye.

5. For hanger, fold $1/2$" x 3" green felt piece in half; glue ends to top back of red felt piece.

6. Center green felt piece, then poster board on gold felt piece and glue in place; center red, then black felt piece over poster board; glue in place.

ROLY-POLY PAL

*Y*ou won't have to wait for snow to create this frosty fellow! An adorable addition to the tree, the playful snowman gets his roly-poly shape from batting and fiberfill. Just add beads, buttons, and a toothpick nose; then wrap him up with a dashing fabric-scrap scarf. Don't forget to top him off with a cap made from the cuff of a child's sock!

FROSTY SNOWMAN

You will need a 12" x 16" piece of batting, white and red embroidery floss, polyester fiberfill, red child-size sock, hot glue gun, craft knife, orange marker, round toothpick, small twigs for arms, two 5mm black beads, black thread, three $1/4$" dia. black buttons, and a $1 1/4$" x 10" torn fabric strip.

1. For body, sew long edges of batting together to form a tube. Use white floss to tightly tie one end of tube closed (bottom); turn right side out. Stuff body with fiberfill. Use white floss to tie top end closed.

2. Tie white floss around snowman to form neck.

3. For hat, turn sock wrong side out. Mark sock 4" from top edge of cuff. Tightly knot a length of red floss around sock at mark. Cut foot from sock $1/2$" below floss; discard foot. Turn hat right side out. Fold edge up to form cuff. Place hat on head and glue in place.

4. Using craft knife, cut a small opening in each side of body for arms and another in face for nose. Using marker, color one end of toothpick for nose. Cut 1" from painted end of toothpick. Glue nose and twigs for arms in openings.

5. Glue beads to face for eyes.

6. Using black thread, sew buttons to front of snowman. Knot fabric strip around neck for scarf.

7. For hanger, take a stitch through top of hat with a 9" length of red floss; knot ends together.

FOLKSY FABRIC STARS

*D*ecked in a constellation of folksy fabric stars, your Christmas tree will illuminate the holidays with homespun cheer! The appliquéd stars are sewn to felt backing using primitive blanket stitches and are slightly stuffed for fullness. Mismatched buttons add charm.

FOLK-ART STARS

For each ornament, you will need paper-backed fusible web, 8" square of fabric, two 8" squares of felt, embroidery floss, polyester fiberfill, ³/₄" dia. button, needle nose pliers, black craft wire, wire cutters, and raffia.

1. Using pattern, page 110, follow *Making Appliqués*, page 124, to make one star appliqué from fabric. Fuse star to center of one felt piece.

2. Matching edges, place felt pieces together. Sewing through all layers, use three strands of embroidery floss to work primitive *Blanket Stitches*, page 125, along edges of appliqué star. Cut out star ¹/₄" outside stitching.

3. Cut a small opening in back layer of felt at center back of ornament. Stuff star with fiberfill; stitch opening closed.

4. Working through all layers, use embroidery floss to sew button to center of star.

5. (*Note*: Use pliers as needed to bend and shape wire.) Use wire cutters to cut a 20" length of craft wire; form a loop at center for hanging loop. Wrap wire ends around a pencil to curl. Push wire ends from back to front through layers on two points of star; bend ends to secure.

6. Tie raffia into a bow around hanging loop.

COUNTRY SANTA

If you've got a pair of worn-out gardening gloves, don't throw them out! This clever little elf is made using a pair of dyed canvas gloves. He's a perfect fit for a country Christmas theme.

GARDEN GLOVE SANTA

You will need a pair of ecru canvas work gloves with knit cuffs, red and black acrylic paint, large glass bowl, hot glue gun, polyester fiberfill, tracing paper, black fabric, muslin, ecru plush felt, small paintbrush, ecru thread, four small ecru buttons, 12" length of 1¼"w ecru cotton fringe, ³/₈" dia. red ball button, black fabric marker, 1¹/₈" dia. ecru shank button, three small red buttons, 9" length of natural raffia, 2½" dia. artificial wreath, and an 18" length of black 20-gauge wire.

1. To dye gloves, mix one ounce red paint and 2½ cups of water in bowl. Soak gloves until desired color is achieved; allow to dry. Cut cuffs from gloves; set aside.

2. For pants, tuck thumb and two outer fingers to inside of one glove. Fold in sides and glue in place (Fig. 1). Stuff pants with fiberfill.

Fig. 1

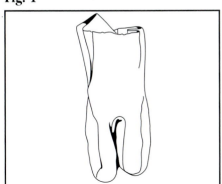

3. Trace patterns, page 108, onto tracing paper. Using patterns, cut four boot shapes from black fabric and two head shapes from muslin.

4. Leaving top edge open and using a ¼" seam allowance, sew each pair of boot shapes together; clip curves and turn right side out. Stuff boots with fiberfill; glue to ends of pant legs.

5. For each pant cuff, cut a ⁵/₈"w strip of felt to fit around pant leg. Glue cuffs around tops of boots.

6. For coat, tuck thumb to inside of second glove. Cut away two middle fingers, to create neck opening. For arms, stuff remaining fingers with fiberfill. Referring to Fig. 2, position arms, pleating fabric as necessary, and glue in place.

Fig. 2

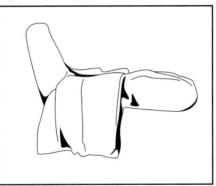

7. For mittens, paint ends of arms black; allow to dry.

8. For each sleeve cuff, cut a ³/₈"w strip of felt to fit around arm. Glue cuffs to arms over tops of mittens.

9. Leaving bottom edge open and using a ¼" seam allowance, sew head shapes together; clip curves and turn right side out. Stuff head with fiberfill. Glue head into neck opening, pleating fabric of neck opening as necessary to fit.

10. For coat trim, cut ⁵/₈"w strips of felt to fit around neck and bottom edges of coat and down front of coat; glue in place.

11. Use ecru thread to sew small ecru buttons to coat trim.

12. For beard and hair, cut a length of fringe to fit around head. Beginning and ending at center back, glue fringe in place. Cut two pieces of fringe for mustache; glue in place.

13. Glue red ball button to face for nose. Use black marker to draw eyes. Cut pieces of fringe for eyebrows; glue in place.

14. For hat, work a *Running Stitch*, page 126, along one raw edge of one removed cuff. Pull thread tightly to gather; knot and trim ends. Glue 1¹/₈" dia. button over gathers. Place hat on head, pleating at back to fit; glue in place. For trim, cut a ³/₄"w strip of felt to fit around head; glue in place over edge of hat.

15. Lightly stuff coat with fiberfill; glue to top of pants.

16. Glue small red buttons to wreath. Tie raffia into a bow; trim ends, and glue to wreath. Glue wreath to one arm.

17. For hanger, curl sections of wire around a pencil. Push ends of wire into back of head; bend to hold in place.

COZY GARLAND

*A*dd a cozy country touch with these stockings and mittens. You can create the festive decorations in no time using crew socks and fabric scraps. Clip them to a length of jute for a fun garland!

COZY STOCKINGS AND MITTENS

For each stocking, you will need tracing paper, two 6" x 8" pieces of fabric, 1" x 6" torn strip of muslin, embroidery floss, 12" length of jute twine, and a 1" dia. wooden button.

For each mitten, you will need tracing paper, adult-size crew sock, two 1³/₈" x 1³/₄" torn fabric pieces, hot glue gun, ³/₄" dia. button, and a 12" length of jute twine.

1. For stocking, trace pattern, page 114, onto tracing paper. Placing fabric pieces right sides together, use pattern to cut out stocking front and back. Leaving top open, use a ¹/₄" seam allowance to sew stocking front and back together. Clip curves; turn stocking right side out and press.

2. Press top edge of stocking ¹/₂" to outside.

3. For cuff, match one raw edge of muslin strip to folded top edge of stocking; use 3 strands of floss and a Running Stitch, page 126, to sew cuff in place ¹/₄" from matched edges.

4. For hanger, fold jute in half. Using embroidery floss and catching jute in stitching, sew button to top back edge of cuff.

5. For mitten, trace pattern, page 113, onto tracing paper.

6. Cut sock along back fold from top edge to toe seam. With right sides together, fold sock as shown in Fig. 1; use pattern to cut out mitten front and back (back will be ¹/₂" longer at cuff than front).

Fig. 1

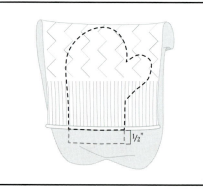

7. Fold excess ¹/₂" at mitten back cuff to wrong side and glue in place.

8. With right sides together and leaving top open, use a ¹/₄" seam allowance to sew mitten front and back together. Clip curves; turn mitten right side out and press.

9. Glue fabric pieces and button to front of mitten.

10. For hanger, fold jute in half. Knot center of jute. Glue knot to top corner of mitten.

LOVING STITCHES

*C*ross stitched with love, these darling ornaments will add a personal touch to special gift packages. The quick-to-make designs are accented with glass seed beads for added dimension.

BEADED CROSS STITCH ORNAMENTS
For each ornament, you will need embroidery floss and seed beads (see color key, page 123); a 5" square of ecru Aida (14 ct); fabric stiffener, $1/16$"w, $1/8$"w, and $3/8$"w; and satin ribbon; and a hot glue gun.

Refer to Cross Stitch and Embroidery instructions, page 125, for Step 1.

1. Referring to chart and color key, page 123, and using three strands of floss for Cross Stitch and one for Backstitch, French Knots, and Attaching Beads, center and work desired design on Aida. Trim Aida to 1" from stitched design.

2. Apply fabric stiffener to back of stitched pieces. Matching wrong sides, place stitched piece on muslin and smooth together; allow to dry. Apply stiffener to back of muslin and allow to dry. Cut out stitched piece close to edges of each design.

3. For angel, cut two 3" lengths of $1/16$"w ribbon. Tie one length into a bow and glue to angel's hand. Glue one end of remaining ribbon length to back of angel's hand; glue other ribbon end to top back of heart. For gingerbread boy, tie $1/8$"w ribbon into a bow and glue to front of gingerbread boy. For wreath, cut a 3" length of $3/8$"w ribbon and tie into a bow; glue bow to wreath.

CUTE & CLEVER

*F*un and festive, merry and bright: these clever ornaments will be a delight! This collection is filled with one-of-a-kind decorations designed to awaken the child in each of us. Bring a favorite character to life with a ruby-nosed sock reindeer, or give Santa a "new" look with a painted flowerpot hat and a crinkled paper beard! You can recapture fond childhood memories with a nostalgic pinwheel tree topper, craft whimsical flocked muslin ornaments, or give a tiny bear a belly full of treats. Set your imagination free!

MERRY "CHRIS-MOUSE"

Twas the night before Christmas, and all through the house…festive cheer could be found with three merry mice! The adorable creatures are crafted from painted holiday light bulbs and nestled in a matchbox bed, a stocking, and a mug. You can hang them on the tree or display them around the house just for fun.

CHRISTMAS MICE

For each ornament, you will need tracing paper; grey craft foam; scraps of assorted fabrics; a large Christmas light bulb; grey acrylic paint; paintbrush; hot glue gun; ecru, brown, and black embroidery floss; black permanent pen; needle nose pliers; 1/4" dia. black shank button; and grey yarn.

For matchbox mouse, you will also need polyester fiberfill, lace trim, and large matchbox.

For stocking mouse, you will also need red and green embroidery floss, toddler-size sock, and polyester fiberfill.

For hot cocoa mouse, you will also need a green paint pen, white teacup, lightweight cardboard, brown felt, and three miniature marshmallows.

1. Trace patterns, page 118, onto tracing paper; cut out. For each mouse, use patterns to cut two ears and two paws from craft foam and one hat from fabric.

2. Paint light bulb grey; allow to dry.

3. To form hat, overlap straight edges and glue in place. For tassel, cut three 2" lengths of ecru floss; place lengths together and knot in center. Glue tassel to tip of hat.

4. For hair, cut several 1/2" lengths of brown floss; separate strands. Glue hat over socket end of bulb; glue hair under edge of hat.

5. Glue ears and paws to head. Use black pen to draw eyes and claws. Use pliers to remove shank from button; glue button to face for nose.

6. For whiskers, cut two 1" lengths of black floss; separate into strands. Place four strands together; glue one end to one side of face. Repeat for remaining side.

7. For tail, cut a 3" length of yarn; knot one end.

Matchbox Mouse

1. For pillow, cut a 2½" x 4" piece from fabric. Matching wrong sides and short edges, fold fabric in half. Glue two sides of pillow together. Stuff pillow lightly with fiberfill through remaining open edge; glue closed. Glue a length of lace along each short end of pillow. Open matchbox about 1"; glue pillow in opening.

2. For blanket, cut a 3½" square from fabric; glue a length of lace along one edge of square. Cut a 3/4" square from fabric for patch; glue to blanket.

3. Place blanket on matchbox; tuck raw edges to wrong side and glue in place.

4. Position mouse head and tail on pillow in matchbox; glue in place.

Stocking Mouse

1. Cut pieces of fabric to fit toe and heel of sock; cut a 3/4" square for patch. Arrange fabric pieces on sock and glue in place.

2. Use three strands of floss to work Straight Stitches, page 126, around edges of patch and straight edges of heel and toe.

3. Stuff sock lightly with fiberfill. Roll top edge of sock cuff down. Arrange mouse head and tail in sock opening; glue in place.

Hot Cocoa Mouse

1. Use green paint pen to write "Merry Chrismouse" on teacup; allow to dry.

2. Draw around teacup opening on cardboard; cut out 1/8" inside drawn line. Cut a circle from felt 1/2" larger all around than cardboard circle. Center cardboard on felt. Clip edges of felt; fold to wrong side of cardboard and glue in place.

3. Place circle in teacup and glue in place. Arrange marshmallows and mouse head and tail on circle; glue in place.

4. Tie a 1" x 12" torn fabric strip into a bow around teacup handle.

PEPPY PINWHEEL

A childhood favorite, colorful pinwheels bring back carefree memories of ice-cream trucks, jump ropes, and sandboxes. Our peppy pinwheel tree topper is perfect for adding a touch of nostalgia to your holiday decor!

PINWHEEL TREE TOPPER

You will need red spray paint, a 12" length of ⁵/₈" dia. wooden dowel, spray adhesive, two 8¹/₂" x 11" sheets of decorative paper, hammer, flat-head straight pin, wire cutters, hot glue gun, and a ¹/₂" dia. jingle bell.

1. Paint dowel red; allow to dry.

2. Apply spray adhesive to backs of both sheets of paper; press sheets together. Cut a 6" square from layered paper.

3. Mark center of paper square. Cut diagonally from each corner of square to 1" from center of square.

4. To form pinwheel, fold every other point to center of square, overlapping points at center. Use hammer to drive pin through overlapped corners, square center, and into dowel. Use wire cutters to cut off sharp end of pin at back of dowel.

5. Hot glue bell to center of pinwheel.

CUTOUT CUTIES

*S*imple poster board-backed muslin cutouts make clever adornments. We chose Santa and sheep shapes to paint, then added soft texture with flocking.

FLOCKED ORNAMENTS

You will need paper-backed fusible web; muslin; poster board; transfer pencil; tracing paper; white, peach, gold, red, green, grey, and black acrylic paint; paintbrushes; white Plaid® Soft Flock®; black fine-point fabric marker; 1/8"w green satin ribbon; and a hot glue gun.

Refer to Painting Basics, page 124, before beginning project. Allow paint and Soft Flock to dry after each application.

1. Use fusible web to fuse muslin to poster board.

2. Following manufacturer's instructions, use transfer pencil to trace desired pattern, page 117, and transfer design to fused muslin. Cut out ornament 1/8" outside design.

3. For sheep, paint ears, face, and legs grey; shade with black. Paint leaves green and berries red. Follow manufacturer's instructions to apply Soft Flock to body and tail. Use marker to draw eyes and nose and outline all parts of design.

4. For Santa, paint face peach, hat and berries red, hat trim and pom-pom gold, and leaves green. Highlight pom-pom with white. Shade hat with black, hair with grey, and nose with red. Follow manufacturer's instructions to apply Soft Flock to beard and mustache. Use marker to draw eyes and outline all parts of design.

5. For each hanger, cut a 14" length of ribbon. Leaving a loop for hanging, tie ribbon ends into a bow. Glue bow to top of ornament.

TERRIFIC TRIO

These snowmen are guaranteed not to melt, but be careful — with their adorable smiles and cheery faces, they might just melt your heart! To make this terrific trio, cover foam balls with artificial snow; then add buttons, twigs, and craft foam to create their jolly faces. To complete your tree in frosty style, craft a flurry of glistening beaded snowflakes, too.

SNOWMAN TRIO

You will need craft sticks, textured glitter snow medium, three 3" dia. plastic foam balls, small wooden skewers, orange acrylic paint, small paintbrush, six small black buttons, black embroidery floss, hot glue gun, craft knife, black craft foam, toddler-size red sock, artificial holly sprigs, clear nylon thread, drawing compass, scraps of assorted fabrics, white and red chenille stems, and one 3/4" dia. white and two 1 3/4" dia. green pom-poms.

Place ornament on a cup while working. Allow textured snow and paint to dry after each application.

1. Use craft stick to apply a thick layer of snow to each ball.

2. For each nose, use craft knife to cut a 1" long piece from pointed end of skewer. Paint nose orange. Apply glue to flat end of nose and push into ball.

3. For each eye, thread one button with floss; knot and trim ends at back. Glue two eyes to each ball.

4. For each mouth, cut five irregularly shaped pieces from foam; glue to ball.

5. For snowman with toboggan cap, fold cuff of sock 1" to right side. Place cap on snowman; glue in place. Glue holly to cuff and white pom-pom to tip of cap.

6. For snowman with top hat, use compass to draw 1 7/8" and 3" dia. circles on craft foam; cut out. Cut a 1 1/2" x 6 1/4" strip from foam; glue short ends together to form a tube. Center and glue foam circles to opposite ends of tube. Glue hat to snowman. Glue holly to hat. Tie a 1" x 9" torn fabric strip into a bow; glue to snowman for scarf.

7. For snowman with earmuffs, cut one 7" length from each chenille stem; twist lengths together. Glue ends of stems to sides of snowman head; glue green pom-poms in place over stem ends. Overlapping ends at front, glue a 5/8" x 9" fabric strip around snowman for scarf. Knot the center of a 5/8" x 4" fabric strip; glue knot to overlap of scarf.

8. For each hanger, take a small stitch through top of cap, hat, or earmuffs with a 9" length of thread; knot ends together.

BEADED SNOWFLAKES

For each ornament, you will need three 12" long white chenille stems, hot glue gun, twelve iridescent white pony beads, 36 clear 6mm faceted beads, six clear sunburst beads, six iridescent white heart beads, and a 9" length of clear nylon thread.

1. Cut three 6" and six 3" pieces from chenille stems.

2. Twist centers of 6" stems together to form a six-pointed star shape. Apply hot glue to back of twist to secure. Thread beads onto each stem end in the following order: white pony, clear faceted, clear sunburst, white pony, clear faceted, and white heart.

3. Twist center of one 3" long stem around each point after heart bead, then add one more clear faceted bead. Form ends of 3" stem into a "V" shape. Touching end of stem lightly with glue, add final clear faceted bead to end of each point.

4. For hanger, knot ends of thread together; glue knot to back of ornament.

PERKY PAINTBRUSH PAL

Crafted from an ordinary paintbrush, this festive fellow will add a "stroke" of Christmas cheer wherever he's displayed! A wooden heart forms his friendly face.

PAINTBRUSH SANTA

You will need tracing paper; transfer paper; stylus; 3"w flat wooden heart; white, red, brown, and black acrylic paint; small paintbrushes; 2½" length of sisal rope; hot glue gun; pinking shears; 9" x 12" piece of red felt; 2"w paintbrush; batting; and a sprig of artificial mistletoe.

1. Trace face pattern, page 103, onto tracing paper. Use transfer paper and stylus to transfer design to heart. Paint eyes and nose; use black to outline eyes and draw lashes and mouth. Highlight eyes and nose with white. Lightly paint cheeks red.

2. For mustache, separate strands of sisal; place together in a bundle. Knot one strand of sisal around center of bundle. Glue bundle to face under nose.

3. Use pinking shears to cut a strip of felt to fit around metal band on 2"w paintbrush; glue in place. Cut remainder of felt into ½"w strips. Overlapping slightly and gluing in place, wrap handle with felt strips. Thread one strip through hole in handle and glue in place to form hanging loop.

4. For hat trim, form a 1" x 7" piece of batting into a roll; glue in place around face. Glue one felt strip along top of hat trim. Glue face to paintbrush.

5. Glue mistletoe to handle.

CLEVER CLASSICS

You'll love these clever trims! They look like the expensive, hand-painted ceramic ornaments you find in department stores, but they're actually easy and inexpensive to make — and durable, too! We decoupaged paper motifs to the insides of clear plastic balls, then added a coat of paint and ribbon accents.

REVERSE DECOUPAGE ORNAMENTS

For each ornament, you will need a 3" dia. clear plastic ball ornament, small foam brushes, decoupage medium, Christmas motifs cut or torn from tissue paper or paper napkin, white acrylic paint, 1/8"w satin ribbon, and a hot glue gun.

1. Separate halves of ornament.

2. Use foam brush to apply decoupage medium to inside of each ornament half; place paper motif right side down in medium. Use foam brush to smooth motif in place; allow to dry.

3. Paint inside of each ornament half white; allow to dry.

4. Reassemble ornament. Thread an 11" length of ribbon through hanger tab on ornament; knot ends together. Tie an 8" length of ribbon into a bow; glue to tab.

HOLIDAY HERALD

Herald the season with this sweet clothespin angel! With her dainty eyelet robe, lace wings, and painted golf-tee trumpet, she's sure to win your heart. Use one ornament to dress up a wreath or package, or craft a heavenly host for the tree.

TRUMPETING ANGEL

You will need a 4" long wooden clothespin; 3/4" dia. wooden bead; utility scissors; craft stick; peach, gold, and black acrylic paint; paintbrushes; wooden golf tee; an 8½" length of 3¾"w white eyelet trim; white thread; hot glue gun; two 3" lengths of 2"w white eyelet trim; embroidery floss; an 11" length of 2"w white lace trim; gold chenille stem; and a 9" length of clear nylon thread.

1. Paint clothespin, bead, and craft stick peach; allow to dry. Glue bead to top of clothespin. Paint black dots on bead for eyes. Using utility scissors, cut a 1" length from each end of craft stick for arms.

2. For trumpet, cut pointed tip from golf tee; paint tee gold and allow to dry.

3. For dress, press unfinished edge and one cut end of 3¾"w eyelet ½" to wrong side. Work a Running Stitch, page 126, along long pressed edge; pull thread, gathering edge to fit around top of clothespin. Knot and trim thread. At back of angel, overlap pressed end of trim over remaining cut edge; glue in place.

4. For each sleeve, use Running Stitch to gather one long edge of each 2"w eyelet piece. Overlap and glue cut edges together. Insert one arm into each sleeve; glue in place. Glue top of sleeves to sides of dress.

5. Glue golf tee in place for trumpet.

6. For hair, cut sixteen 4" lengths of floss; place lengths together to form bundle. Tie another 4" length of floss loosely around center of bundle. Arrange hair on head and glue in place.

7. For wings, fold lace trim to form a loop, overlapping ends 2". Wrap thread around center; knot to secure. Glue center of wings to back of angel.

8. For halo, cut a 4" length from chenille stem; form into a circle, twisting ends at overlap. Glue halo to back of head.

9. For hanger, knot ends of nylon thread together; glue knot to back of ornament.

ALL HEART

*F*or a character who's "all heart," craft a jolly Santa face from a Shaker box! His fluffy beard is really textured snow, and his felt hat is a snap to stitch together. You can even fill the box with treats to surprise a friend!

HEARTY SANTA

You will need a 2¹⁄₂" x 2¹⁄₂" heart-shaped Shaker box, white and peach acrylic paint, paintbrushes, red and black fine-point pens, craft stick, textured snow medium, tracing paper, white and red felt, hot glue gun, a ³⁄₄" dia. jingle bell, and a 9" length of clear nylon thread.

Allow paint and textured snow to dry after each application.

1. Use a pencil to lightly sketch an outline of face on lid near point of box. Paint face peach. Using black pen, draw details on face and color eyes; using red pen, color nose, mouth, and cheeks. Using tip of paintbrush handle, paint white highlights in eyes.

2. Following manufacturer's instructions and using craft stick, apply textured snow to Santa for beard.

3. Trace pattern, page 123, onto tracing paper. Using pattern, cut hat from red felt. For hat trim, cut a ¹⁄₂" x 4" strip from white felt.

4. Sew straight edges of hat together. Glue hat trim along bottom edge of hat. Stitch bell to tip of hat. Place hat on Santa; glue in place.

5. For hanger, knot ends of nylon thread together; glue knot to back of ornament.

FROSTY FRAME

*D*isplay *a favorite photograph in this frosty frame! Our friendly snowman makes a great tree trimmer or package decoration, as well as a welcome gift for proud grandparents.*

BABY'S FIRST CHRISTMAS

You will need a 3¹/₂" dia. white plastic picture frame; photograph to fit in frame; tracing paper; white, orange, green, and black craft foam; hot glue gun; white chenille stem; two ³/₄" dia. red pom-poms; two craft picks; white acrylic paint; paintbrush; 1¹/₂" x 16" torn fabric strip; and a 3" length of white craft wire.

1. Follow frame manufacturer's instructions to mount photo in frame.

2. Trace patterns, page 120, onto tracing paper; cut out. Using patterns, cut nose from orange foam, two mittens from green foam, a 2¹/₄" dia. circle for head from white foam, and six irregularly shaped pieces for eyes and mouth from black foam.

3. Glue eyes, nose, and mouth to head; glue head to top of frame. For earmuffs, cut a 4¹/₂" length from chenille stem; bend to fit across top of head and glue in place. Glue one pom-pom over each end of stem.

4. Paint craft picks white; cut a 2¹/₂" length from each pick. Glue one end of each pick to a mitten; glue opposite end to back of frame.

5. For scarf, tie fabric strip around neck and glue in place.

6. For hanger, fold wire to form a loop; glue ends to back of ornament.

Who would've guessed such clever ornaments could be made from craft spoons! You can even let the kids help — have a grown-up do the cutting, and the youngsters can have fun assembling colorful poinsettias and whimsical reindeer trios. What cute ideas!

CRAFT-SPOON POINSETTIA

You will need a utility scissors, eight red and three green wooden craft spoons, hot glue gun, assorted small white and yellow beads, and a 9" length of clear nylon thread.

1. Use utility scissors to cut handles from green spoons and from four red spoons; discard handles. Glue one red spoon half to handle of each whole red spoon (Fig. 1).

Fig. 1

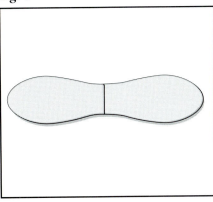

2. Glue one pair of red spoons together to form a cross; repeat with second pair. Layer and glue red spoons and green spoon halves to form poinsettia.

3. Glue beads in place to form flower center.

4. For hanger, knot ends of thread together to form a loop; glue knot to back of ornament.

SPOON REINDEER TRIO

You will need three 12" long brown chenille stems, hot glue gun, one red and two green wooden craft spoons, black fine-point pen, three 6mm black pom-poms, red and green small craft sticks, red and green embroidery floss, three 9mm jingle bells, and a 9" length of clear nylon thread.

1. Referring to Fig. 1, bend each chenille stem to form one set of ears and antlers; glue in place on one side of each spoon.

Fig. 1

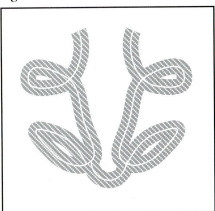

2. Use pen to draw eyes and mouth on each spoon. For nose, glue one pom-pom to each face.

3. Glue craft sticks to back of reindeer.

4. Use embroidery floss to tie one bell to each reindeer's neck.

5. For hanger, knot ends of thread together to form a loop; glue knot to back of ornament.

TANTALIZING TREE TREATS

Transform your tree into a tantalizing treat that even Santa won't be able to resist! A clear plastic ornament filled with goodies forms our bear's tummy, and the sweet garland is made by gluing wrapped candies and wired-ribbon bows to lengths of cord.

CANDY TEDDY BEAR AND GARLAND
You will need utility scissors, a 3" dia. clear plastic ball ornament, hot glue gun, teddy bear parts, a 16" length of 7/8"w wired ribbon, large needle, 1/16" dia. gold braid, 1/8" dia. decorative cord, wrapped red and green candies, and red and green 1/8"w satin ribbon.

1. Use utility scissors to cut hanging tab from top of ornament.

2. Glue teddy bear head, arms, and legs to back section of ornament. With candy inside, place ornament halves together.

3. Tie wired ribbon into a bow around bear's neck.

4. For hanger, use needle to take a small stitch with gold braid in top of bear's head. Knot ends of braid together.

5. For garland, knot ends of cord. Cut satin ribbon into 8" lengths; tie each into a bow.

6. Alternating colors, glue bows and candy to cord.

AMERICA'S FAVORITE REINDEER

Celebrate the holidays with America's favorite reindeer! Radiating a cheery glow, our character is created with a pair of children's socks, fiberfill, and felt. And for that oh-so-famous nose, glue on a bright red pom-pom.

SOCK REINDEER

You will need a pair of child-size tan socks, polyester fiberfill, tracing paper, red and brown felt, two 3¹/₂" lengths of 20-gauge wire, hot glue gun, pinking shears, green baby rickrack, two small black buttons, a 1" dia. red pom-pom, three 12mm jingle bells, and a 9" length of clear nylon thread.

1. Stuff one sock with fiberfill. To close sock opening, work a Running Stitch, page 126, ¹/₂" from top edge of sock; pull thread tightly to gather. Wrap thread several times around gathers; take a stitch and knot and trim thread. Bend sock at ankle to form neck; stitch in place.

2. Trace ear and antler patterns, page 110, onto tracing paper; cut out.

3. Placing ear pattern on fold, cut two ears from second sock. Stitch curved edges of each ear together. Stitch short edge of one ear to each side of head.

4. Using antler pattern, cut four antlers from brown felt. For each antler, center and glue a length of wire between two antler pieces. Glue ends of antlers to top of head.

5. For bridle, use pinking shears to cut a ¹/₂"w strip of red felt to fit around muzzle; glue in place. For collar, cut a 1"w strip of red felt to fit around neck; glue in place. Cut rickrack to fit around bridle; glue in place.

6. For reins, cut a length of rickrack to fit loosely around back of head. Tuck ends of reins under bridle; glue to secure. Glue center of reins to back of head.

7. Glue buttons to head for eyes and pom-pom to head for nose. Glue bells to collar.

8. For hanger, take a small stitch at top of head with nylon thread. Knot thread ends together.

SANTA'S LITTLE STAR

*L*et your favorite little "star" shine in this stellar ornament! Perfect for showing off that special boy or girl, our photo ornament is made using cardboard, batting, and felt. Gold twisted cord neatly frames the adornment, and a festive little Santa hat makes the youngster the center of attention!

PHOTO IMAGE SANTA STAR

You will need tracing paper, white and red felt, batting, cardboard, color photograph, photo transfer paper, 10" square of white fabric, red dimensional fabric paint, craft glue, a 30" length of ³/₁₆" dia. gold twisted cord, and a 5mm jingle bell.

Allow craft glue to dry after each application.

1. Trace hat, hat trim, and star patterns, page 109, onto tracing paper; cut out. Using patterns, cut hat from red felt, hat trim from white felt, and one star each from batting, cardboard, and white felt.

2. Have color photograph copied onto transfer paper at copy center. Cut desired image from transfer. Follow manufacturer's instructions to transfer image to center of white fabric.

3. Referring to Fig. 1, position star pattern on fabric over transferred photo, leaving room for hat. Lightly draw around pattern on fabric; cut out star 1" outside drawn line.

Fig. 1

4. Glue batting star to cardboard star; center glued stars batting side down on wrong side of fabric star. Clipping fabric at inner points, wrap fabric edges to back of cardboard star and glue in place. Glue felt star to back of cardboard star, covering fabric edges.

5. Apply dots of paint along edges of ornament front; allow to dry.

6. To prevent fraying, apply craft glue to ends of cord; allow to dry.

7. Beginning at top, glue cord along edges of ornament, forming a 2" hanging loop at top of star; glue end of cord to back of ornament.

8. Sew jingle bell to tip of hat; glue hat and hat trim to ornament.

KRISS "KRINKLE"

Santa will be full of smiles when he sees this delightful decoration hanging on the tree! Our jolly ornament is so easy to make: just paint a papier-mâché ornament and glue on crinkle paper for the beard, hair, and eyebrows. And don't forget his hat — a painted flowerpot!

KRISS "KRINKLE"

You will need a 2³/₄" dia. flowerpot; white, peach, and red acrylic paint; paintbrushes; stencil brush; 3" dia. papier-mâché ball ornament; hot glue gun; two straight pins with ¹/₈" dia. black bead heads; ³/₈" dia. red bead; pink marker; and shredded white crinkle paper.

Allow paint to dry after each application.

1. For hat, paint flowerpot red. Paint rim white; use stencil brush and white paint to add texture to rim of pot. Paint papier-mâché ball peach.

2. Threading ornament hanger through opening in bottom of pot, glue pot to top of ornament.

3. Insert pins into ornament for eyes. Glue bead in place for nose. Use marker to draw mouth.

4. Glue crinkle paper to ornament for hair, eyebrows, and beard and to top of hat for pom-pom.

FUNNY FELLOW

Even Scrooge would have to smile at this funny fellow! With his wooden heart body, baggy trousers, and button beard, he'll add a touch of whimsy to the evergreen.

HANDCRAFTED SANTA

You will need utility scissors; craft stick; gold, red, light green, green, light brown, brown, and black acrylic paint; paintbrushes; two 1³/₄" wooden boot cutouts; 2¹/₂" tall wooden Christmas tree cutout; 1" x 1", 1¹/₂" x 1¹/₂", and 3" x 4" wooden heart cutouts; tracing paper; scraps of red fabric; spray adhesive; two 2¹/₂" long clothespins; polyester fiberfill; hot glue gun; pinking shears; white plush felt; two white sequins; one red and two black seed beads; white doll hair; white thread; assorted small white buttons; ¹/₂"w black grosgrain ribbon; ¹/₂" dia. gold button for buckle; red and black embroidery floss; and craft wire.

Allow paint to dry after each application.

1. Use utility scissors to cut craft stick in half; discard one half. Paint remaining half, large and small hearts, and clothespins red. Paint boots black.

2. Use green and light green paint to paint tree; paint trunk brown. Referring to photo, use tip of small brush to paint details on tree and small heart.

3. Draw around large heart on tracing paper; cut out. Fold paper heart in half horizontally; cut along crease and discard lower half. Using upper half for pattern, cut two shapes from fabric. Use spray adhesive to attach fabric shapes to front and back of wooden heart.

4. Referring to Fig. 1, arrange large heart, unpainted heart, and craft stick half to form body; glue in place. Glue clothespins to body for arms.

Fig. 1

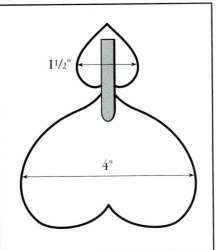

5. Trace hat pattern, page 118, onto tracing paper. Using pattern, cut hat from fabric. Matching wrong sides, fold hat in half and sew straight edges together to form cone. Turn hat right side out; stuff lightly with fiberfill. Glue hat on head.

6. For hat trim, use pinking shears to cut a ¹/₄" x 4" strip from felt. Glue strip around bottom of hat, cutting off excess. Roll remainder of strip to form pom-pom; glue on hat.

7. Glue sequins and seed beads to face for eyes and nose. Dry brush cheeks with red paint; paint red mouth on face. Tie center of small bundle of doll hair with white thread; glue in place for mustache. Arrange white buttons to form beard; glue in place.

8. For each pant leg, cut a 4" square from fabric. Matching right sides, fold square in half. Using a ¹/₄" seam allowance, sew long edges together to form a tube; turn right side out. To gather ends, flatten tube and work a Running Stitch, page 126, close to each raw edge. Pull thread to gather; knot and trim thread ends.

9. Glue one end of each pant leg to back of large heart; glue boot cutouts to lower ends of pant legs.

10. For fur trim, use pinking shears to cut ¹/₂"w strips of felt to fit around waist, bottoms of pant legs, wrists, and down front of shirt; glue strips in place.

11. Glue ribbon in place for belt. Thread gold button with black floss; knot at back of button and trim floss ends. Glue button in place for belt buckle.

12. Cut two 1¹/₄" lengths of craft wire; glue to top backs of small heart and tree cutouts. Glue opposite ends of wire into openings in clothespins.

13. Bend a 5" length of wire to form hanger; glue to back of ornament.

HOLIDAY PRETTIES

*F*or holiday pretties in a flash, cross stitch these ornaments! They're great for package tie-ons or tree trims. Gold cord and red ribbon hangers add a stylish finish.

JOYFUL CROSS STITCH ORNAMENTS
For each ornament, you will need embroidery floss (see color key), 5" square of white Aida (14 ct), low-loft polyester batting, poster board, hot glue gun, ¼"w grosgrain ribbon, and ⅜" gold cord.

Refer to Cross Stitch, page 127, before beginning project.

1. Using three strands of floss for Cross Stitch and one for Backstitch and French Knots, center and work desired design on Aida. For wreath and banner, trim stitched piece to 1" from design. For candle, lightly draw a square around candle on wrong side of Aida; cut out 1" outside square. For backing, cut a piece of fabric same size as stitched piece.

2. Cut two poster board shapes and one batting shape ¹/₂" smaller than stitched piece. Center batting, then one poster board piece, on wrong side of stitched piece. At ¹/₂" intervals, make clips into stitched piece to ¹/₈" from edges of poster board. Alternating sides, glue edges of stitched piece to poster board.

3. Trimming to fit, glue cord along edges of ornament.

4. Center remaining poster board piece on wrong side of backing fabric piece. At ¹/₂" intervals, make clips into stitched piece to ¹/₈" from edges of poster board. Alternating sides, glue edges of fabric to poster board.

5. For hanger, cut a 7" length of ribbon. Glue ends of ribbon to top back of ornament; glue wrong side of backing to back of ornament. Tie a 9" length of ribbon into a bow and glue to front of ornament.

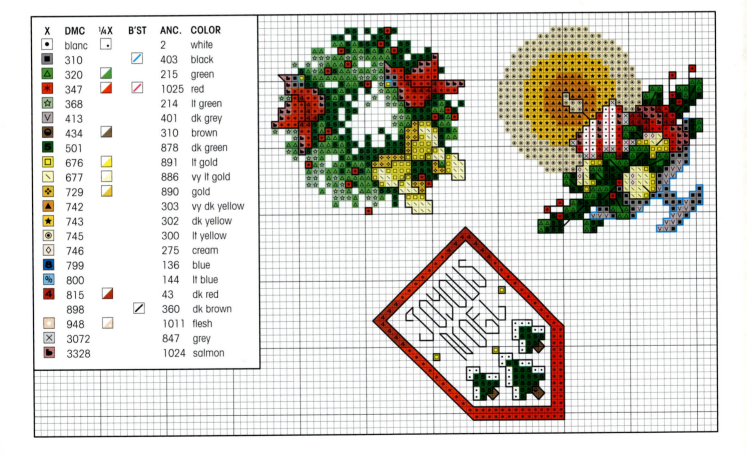

X	DMC	¼X	B'ST	ANC.	COLOR
•	blanc	•		2	white
■	310		/	403	black
△	320	◩		215	green
✳	347	◢	/	1025	red
☆	368			214	lt green
V	413			401	dk grey
◔	434	◥		310	brown
▩	501			878	dk green
▱	676	◩		891	lt gold
◹	677	◱		886	vy lt gold
✿	729	◩		890	gold
▲	742			303	vy dk yellow
★	743			302	dk yellow
◉	745			300	lt yellow
◇	746			275	cream
◙	799			136	blue
%	800			144	lt blue
4	815	◢		43	dk red
	898		/	360	dk brown
▢	948	◸		1011	flesh
✕	3072			847	grey
◗	3328			1024	salmon

TRASH TO TREASURE

*I*s your recycling bin overflowing with hidden treasures? Salvage those fast-food takeout boxes, empty cans, plastic bags, and other throw-aways and put them to good use! Just flip through the following pages and you'll discover a host of holly-jolly trims crafted from — you guessed it — items that would normally go into your trash can! You can transform a burned-out light bulb into a cheerful little penguin, craft a charming Mrs. Claus with a paper-towel-tube body, or disguise a battered tart pan as a colorful photo frame, just to name a few. Don't trash it…treasure it!

You can enjoy the classic look of stained glass for mere pennies with these celestial trims! Our colorful angel and stars began as plastic take-out containers.

FAUX STAINED-GLASS ORNAMENTS
You will need a large clear plastic food container, Gallery Glass™ liquid leading and transparent glass paints, paintbrushes, 1/8" dia. hole punch, a 2 1/2" length of 1/16"w gold braid, and clear nylon thread.

1. Cut flat sections from top and bottom of food container. Placing plastic pieces over patterns, page 103, use liquid leading to trace angel and small star once and large star twice onto plastic; allow to dry.

2. Use glass paint to paint each section in each design; allow to dry. Cut out ornaments along outer line.

3. Use hole punch to make holes in angel hand and small star. Thread one end of gold braid through each hole; knot ends to secure.

4. For hangers, make a hole in top of each large star. Thread a 9" length of nylon thread through each hole; knot ends together.

RECYCLED SANTA

A great project for grade-school children, this simple-to-make Santa is constructed using "recycled" items! For instance, the jolly gent's face begins as a snack chip container lid. Painted pinecone scales are added for his eyes and nose, and foam packing peanuts make up his unruly beard.

RECYCLED SANTA

You will need paintbrushes; 3" dia. lid from a snack chip container; white, beige, red, and black acrylic paint; three scales from a pinecone; low-temperature glue gun; foam packing peanuts; 3¹/₂" x 8" piece of red felt; 7" and 9" long pieces of white chenille stem; and a 9" length of clear nylon thread.

Allow paint to dry after each application.

1. For head, paint top of lid beige. Mix one part red paint with one part water; use mixture to paint a ¹/₂"w red line across center of lid.

2. For eyes, paint two pinecone scales black. For nose, paint remaining scale red. Paint white highlights on eyes and nose. Glue eyes and nose to face. Paint black mouth on face below nose.

3. Trimming as necessary, glue foam peanuts to face for beard, mustache, and eyebrows.

4. With short edges overlapping at back, glue felt around head for hat. Gather top of hat and wrap 7" chenille stem around

gathers to secure; form ends into loops. With ends at back, wrap 9" chenille stem around bottom of hat; twist to secure.

5. For hanger, take a stitch through top back of hat with nylon thread; knot ends together.

MRS. CLAUS

With her jolly smile and pleasant disposition, our Mrs. C. is as delightful as can be! Cleverly crafted from a paper towel tube, the lovely lady is geared up for the cold in a cozy felt dress and her best doily shawl. And with a stocking in her hand, we can guess that she's ready to help Santa as well!

MRS. CLAUS

You will need a paper towel tube; white, pink, red, and black acrylic paint; foam brushes; small paintbrushes; 2$\frac{1}{2}$" dia. papier-mâché ball ornament; 1$\frac{1}{2}$" dia. wooden head bead; 2"w wooden heart cutout; two 5" lengths of 19-gauge black wire; hot glue gun; mop yarn; tracing paper; ecru, tan, gold, and red felt; poster board; $\frac{1}{2}$"w lace trim; two straight pins with red bead heads; pinking shears; embroidery floss; a 5" square doily; and a 5" length of $\frac{1}{2}$"w ribbon.

1. Cut a 2$\frac{1}{2}$" long piece from tube.

2. Allowing paint to dry after each application, paint tube piece and papier-mâché ball red; paint heart black. Paint black eyes and red mouth on bead; use pink paint to add nose and cheeks. Highlight cheeks and eyes with white.

3. Bend one wire length to form eyeglasses; glue ends to sides of head. For hanger, form one end of second wire length into hook shape. Glue opposite end in hole in top of head.

4. For hair, wrap mop yarn around head and into a bun; glue in place.

5. Glue tube to bottom of papier-mâché ball; glue heart to opposite end of tube for feet.

6. Trace patterns, page 101, onto tracing paper. Using patterns, cut two hands from tan felt and two stockings from gold felt. Using pinking shears to cut one long edge, cut a $\frac{1}{2}$" x 2$\frac{1}{4}$" strip of ecru felt for stocking cuff.

7. For arms, cut two $\frac{5}{8}$" x 2$\frac{1}{4}$" pieces of poster board and two 1$\frac{1}{2}$" x 2$\frac{1}{2}$" pieces of red felt.

8. Glue one hand to one end of each poster board piece. Wrap red felt pieces around poster board pieces and glue in place. Cut lace trim to fit around each wrist; glue in place. Use pins with red bead heads to pin top of one arm to each side of ornament.

9. Using pinking shears to cut one long edge, cut four 1$\frac{1}{4}$" x 7$\frac{1}{4}$" strips of red felt for skirt. Beginning at bottom of tube and overlapping strips, glue strips around tube with ends at back, covering tube completely.

10. Matching stocking shapes and using two strands of embroidery floss, work Blanket Stitch, page 125, along side and bottom edges of stocking. Work Straight Stitch, page 126, along pinked edge of cuff. Glue cuff around top of stocking. Glue stocking between hands.

11. Place doily over ornament; glue in place. Position head on ornament over doily; glue in place. Cut lace trim to fit around neck; glue in place.

12. Fold ribbon to form a bow; wrap and tie center with embroidery floss. Glue bow in place at neck.

NOSTALGIC NUTCRACKER

Christmas just wouldn't be complete without a nostalgic nutcracker. Whether you hang yours from the tree or display him on a table, our ornament is the perfect addition to your collection. He's fashioned using an empty paper tube and a tiny flowerpot.

PINT-SIZE NUTCRACKER

You will need a toilet paper tube; white, beige, red, and black acrylic paint; paintbrushes; 2" dia. flowerpot; utility scissors; craft stick; jumbo craft stick; an 8" length of 1/16" dia. gold cord; tracing paper; stylus; transfer paper; gold paint pen; hot glue gun; black fine-point pen; and a 1/2" x 1" piece of white artificial fur.

1. Paint top 1/3 of tube beige, middle 1/3 red, and bottom 1/3 black. Paint flower pot black.

2. Use utility scissors to cut craft stick and jumbo craft stick in half. Paint 1/2" of rounded end of craft stick halves beige; paint remainder red. Paint jumbo craft stick halves black.

3. Paint black belt on red section of tube.

4. For hanger, thread ends of cord through hole to inside of pot. Knot cord ends together and glue knot inside pot. With loop extending through hole, glue pot to head for hat.

5. For feet, glue jumbo craft sticks to bottom of tube. For arms, glue edges of craft sticks to sides of tube.

6. Using patterns, page 122, trace face and jacket details onto tracing paper. Use

stylus and transfer paper to transfer details to tube. Use paints, paint pen, and black pen to paint details.

7. For beard, glue fur piece to face below mouth.

SNAZZY SNOWMAN

*I*t's hard to believe this snazzy little snowman had such humble beginnings! You can easily create our wind sock snowman by sponge painting a tomato paste can white and hand-painting his smiling face. Make the festive streamers from a plastic bag, and keep the fellow snug with bottle cap earmuffs!

WIND SOCK SNOWMAN

You will need a 6-oz. tomato paste can; hammer; small nail; four metal soda bottle caps; white spray primer; natural sponge piece; white, pink, and black PermEnamel™ paint; small paintbrushes; hot glue gun; a 9" length of black craft wire; pencil; white plastic bag; 1" x 12" torn fabric strip; utility knife; small twig; and orange acrylic paint.

Allow primer and paint to dry after each application.

1. Remove bottom from can. Using hammer and nail, punch one hole in each side at top of can. Spray can and bottle caps with primer.

2. Follow Sponge Painting, page 124, to paint can white. Paint bottle caps black. Paint black eyes, eyebrows, and mouth on can. Sponge paint pink cheeks on face.

3. For earmuffs, glue pairs of bottle caps together. Twist wire around a pencil. Insert ends of wire into holes in can from inside; bend to secure. Glue earmuffs over holes.

4. Referring to Fig. 1, cut a 3¼" x 7" strip from bottom of plastic bag. For fringe, make ½"w clips in strip to seamline of bag. Glue fringe to inside bottom edge of can, overlapping ends of strip.

Fig. 1

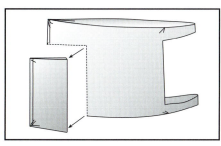

5. For scarf, knot fabric strip around can.

6. For nose, use utility knife to cut a ¾" piece from twig; trim one end of twig to a point. Glue flat end of twig to can. Paint twig and glue at base of twig orange.

"CANNED" COWPOKE

Git along, little dogies! Delight little cowpokes (and big ones, too!) with our adorable "canned" cowboy. This crushed-can character sports craft-foam arms and legs and a jute lariat. For an authentic denim look, use a scrap of canvas to stamp paint his blue jeans.

CRUSHED CAN COWBOY

You will need a 12-oz. aluminum beverage can; white spray primer; white, beige, yellow, khaki, dark khaki, red, brown, light blue, blue, brown, copper, silver, and black acrylic paint; paintbrushes; black fine-point marker; tracing paper; beige craft foam; awl; miniature chili bucket; 3" red flocked cowboy hat; an 18" length of jute twine; scrap of canvas fabric; hot glue gun; clear acrylic spray sealer; and a 6" length of 19-gauge wire.

Refer to Painting Basics, page 124, before beginning project. Allow primer, paint, and sealer to dry after each application.

1. Remove tab from can; set aside. Use both hands to hold can with thumbs below top rim and opening. Using thumbs, press on can to bend top of rim down. Turn can upside down and repeat to bend bottom of can in opposite direction (Fig. 1). Step on can to flatten further.

Fig. 1

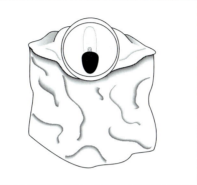

2. Spray can with one coat of primer. Paint visible area inside mouth red. Paint face beige. Dry brush cheeks and nose with red. Using oval hole in can tab as a template, draw eyes on face. Paint eyes white; paint pupils black with white highlights. Use black marker to draw eyelashes and eyebrows.

3. Trace patterns, page 122, onto tracing paper; cut out. Using patterns, cut two hands and two boots from foam. For arms and legs, cut four ½" x 2" pieces from foam.

4. Glue hands to ends of arms; glue top of each arm to can. Glue boots to ends of legs; glue top of each leg to can.

5. Paint arms, boots, and upper half of body red. Use khaki and dark khaki to paint plaid design on shirt.

6. For jeans, paint lower half of body and legs blue. Use canvas piece to lightly stamp with light blue to simulate denim texture.

7. For buckle, paint can tab copper; paint silver dots on buckle.

8. Use brown paint to paint belt. Use blue to paint belt loops over belt. Use yellow to paint stitching on jeans.

9. For hanger, use awl to punch a small hole in top of head. Bend wire end into an "L" shape; glue inside hole. Shape opposite end of wire to form hanger.

10. Coil twine into a 1½" dia. loop; bend fingers of one hand around twine loop and glue in place. Bend fingers of remaining hand around handle of chili bucket and glue in place on front of jeans. Glue buckle to belt.

11. Spray ornament with two coats of acrylic sealer.

12. Cut a small opening in top of hat. Threading hanger through hole, place hat on head; glue to secure.

A BRIGHT IDEA

It's hard to believe this playful little fellow began as a burned-out light bulb! Using craft foam for the wings and tail, simply paint the body and face and add a wooden heart cutout for the feet. What a "bright" idea!

DELIGHTFUL PENGUIN

You will need white spray primer; standard-size light bulb; white, yellow, and black acrylic paint; paintbrushes; 1³/₄"w wooden heart cutout; hot glue gun; infant-size sock; needle and thread; 1" dia. pom-pom; tracing paper; black craft foam, and a 9" length of nylon thread.

Refer to Painting Basics, page 124, before beginning project. Allow primer and paint to dry after each application.

1. Apply primer to light bulb. Use a pencil to lightly sketch outline for tummy and face. Paint tummy and face white. Dry brush edges of tummy and face yellow. Paint remainder of bulb black. Paint eyes black and beak yellow; outline beak with black.

2. For hat, cut cuff from sock. Baste along cut edge of cuff. Pull thread to gather edge; knot ends. Glue pom-pom over gathers. Fold finished edge of cuff ¼" to right side; glue hat over socket end of bulb.

3. For feet, paint heart yellow; glue to bottom of penguin.

4. Trace patterns, page 106, onto tracing paper. Using patterns, cut tail and wings from craft foam. Referring to Fig. 1, glue tail and wings to back of penguin.

Fig. 1

5. For hanger, knot ends of nylon thread together to form loop; glue knot to back of ornament.

PICTURE-PERFECT

Here's a picture-perfect way to showcase your pride and joys! Just cut an ornament shape from a plastic food container lid, glue a photocopy of your favorite picture on the back, and accent with dimensional paint and tissue paper. What a splendid way to add personality to your tree!

ORNAMENTAL PHOTOS

For each ornament, you will need gold dimensional paint, lid from a clear plastic food container, white tissue paper, color photocopy of photograph, craft glue, foam brush, assorted colors of acrylic paint, small paintbrushes, 1/8" dia. hole punch, and a 9" length of heavy gold thread.

Refer to Painting Basics, page 124, before beginning project. Allow paint and glue to dry after each application.

1. For each ornament, place plastic over desired pattern, page 67; tape in place. Use dimensional paint to paint over lines of pattern; allow to dry. Cut out ornament along outer edge of design.

2. Cut a 2" dia. circle from photocopy; glue front of circle to back of ornament.

3. Draw around ornament on tissue paper; cut out. Use craft glue thinned with water to glue paper to back of ornament over photo.

4. Use acrylic paint thinned with water to paint shapes on back of ornament.

5. For hanger, use hole punch to make a hole in top of ornament. Fold thread in half; knot ends together. Place loop through hole and pull knot through loop.

These Yuletide companions will spread the childlike wonder of Christmas wherever you display them! And you can make them using supplies you may already have . . . such as paper sacks, fabric scraps, and poster board. What fun family projects!

RUDY THE REINDEER

You will need a 3" x 5½" brown paper bag, polyester fiberfill, two tan chenille stems, hot glue gun, six ¼" dia. jingle bells, 8" length of ⅛"w ribbon, pliers, ½" dia. red plastic shank button, two ⅝" dia. wiggle eyes, black permanent marker, and a 9" length of clear nylon thread.

1. For hair, make 1" long clips ¼" apart along top of bag.

2. Lightly stuff bag with fiberfill to 2" from top. Gather top of bag over fiberfill.

3. For antlers, with ends at back, tightly twist center of one chenille stem around gathers below hair. Fold hair to front of bag and glue bottom layer of hair to bag. Cut two 3" lengths from remaining chenille stem; wrap one length around each antler. Bend and shape antlers as desired. Glue bells to antlers. Tie ribbon into a bow around bottom of antlers.

4. For nose, use pliers to remove shank from button. Glue nose and eyes to front of bag. Use marker to draw mouth.

5. For hanger, knot ends of nylon thread together. Glue knot to top of bag behind antlers.

ELVIN THE ELF

You will need scraps of assorted fabrics, paper-backed fusible web, 4" x 8" paper bag, polyester fiberfill, glue stick, rubber band, hot glue gun, five ¼" dia. jingle bells, 9" length of ⅛"w ribbon, tracing paper, poster board, scrap of brown paper, black permanent fine-point pen, beige and pink colored pencils, and a 9" length of clear nylon thread.

Use hot glue unless otherwise indicated.

1. Cut 4" x 8" rectangles from fabric and fusible web. Use web to fuse fabric to front of bag. Stuff bag half full with fiberfill. Use glue stick to glue top 2" of bag together. Fold top of bag 2½" to front; use rubber band to form neck below fold line.

2. For collar, cut four points in folded part of bag. Glue bells to points of collar. Tie ribbon into a bow; trim ends. Glue bow to collar. Fold ends of collar to back of bag and glue in place.

3. Tear two ¾" x 5" and two 1" x 7" strips from fabric. Knot each strip near one end; knot 7" strips at centers for knees. Glue unknotted end of one 5" strip to each side of bag for arms; glue unknotted ends of 7" strips to bottom of bag for legs.

4. Trace head and hat trim patterns, page 108, onto tracing paper. Using patterns, cut head from poster board and hat trim from brown paper. Using hat pattern, page 108, and following *Making Appliqués*, page 124, make hat appliqué from fabric. Fuse appliqué to poster board; cut out.

5. Use pen to draw face on head; use colored pencils to color face and cheeks. Glue hat and hat trim to head. Glue remaining jingle bell to top of hat. Glue head to top of collar.

6. For hanger, knot ends of nylon thread together. Glue knot to back of head.

GILDED BEAUTY

This gilded beauty makes an elegant tree topper or table decoration! Her body is crafted from a soda bottle, and her glittering gown is made from painted produce bags.

ANGEL TREE TOPPER

You will need a craft knife, 20-ounce plastic beverage bottle, 2" plastic egg, hot glue gun, utility scissors, two aluminum beverage cans, cutting mat, tracing paper, stylus, two flat wooden ice cream spoons, white spray primer, blue and metallic gold spray paint, metallic gold acrylic paint, toothbrush, two 7" x 11" plastic mesh vegetable bags, gold 20-gauge craft wire, wire cutters, ¹/₂"w gold mesh wired ribbon; and two gold buttons.

1. For body, use craft knife to cut bottom from bottle; glue egg to bottle neck for head.

2. Use utility scissors to cut top and bottom from each can. Cut each can from top to bottom and flatten to form a rectangle.

3. Trace wing pattern, page 112, onto tracing paper; cut out. Using pattern, cut two wings from can rectangles. Place wings on cutting mat or layers of newspaper. Reversing pattern, use stylus and press hard to transfer details to each wing.

4. Spray body, wings, and spoons with primer, then with blue paint. Refer to *Spatter Painting*, page 124, and use gold paint to spatter paint each piece.

5. For dress, cut bottom from one bag to form a tube. For sleeves, cut a 6" x 22" rectangle from remaining bag. Spray each bag section with blue, then gold paint.

6. Place bag for dress over body; use lengths of wire to gather dress around waist and neck. Adjust gathers.

7. For arms, wrap center of an 18" length of wire once around upper body; twist together at back. Glue large end of one wooden spoon to each wire end.

8. To complete dress, place remaining bag piece across front of angel; wrap to back over arms. Fold ends of bag piece 1" to inside at wrists; gather to fit wrists and secure with wire. Adjust gathers across bodice.

9. Wrap a 24" length of ribbon around waist and knot at front of angel. Knot center of an 18" length of ribbon at front of neck; bring ribbon ends down bodice front. Slip one ribbon end under belt; knot ends together at belt. Wrap ribbon ends around a pencil to curl. Glue one button over each knot.

10. For halo, twist two 10" lengths of wire together; form a circle at center of wire. Twist wire ends together to secure and glue to back of angel at neck. Glue wings in place on back of angel.

ANGEL OF GOLD

*Y*ou can enjoy the look of costly burnished metal...without spending a fortune! This "antique" angel is cut from a poster board scrap, detailed with hot glue, and then painted.

ANTIQUED GOLD ANGEL

You will need tracing paper, poster board, hot glue gun, craft stick, gold spray paint, black acrylic paint, paintbrush, a 4" length of gold baby rickrack, and narrow gold braid.

1. Trace angel and star patterns, page 119, onto tracing paper; cut out. Draw around angel pattern once and star pattern three times on poster board.

2. Use hot glue to draw over angel outline and add dots and detail lines to angel and stars. For hair, apply hot glue to head and use craft stick to add texture. Cut out angel and stars.

3. Spray paint angel and stars gold; allow to dry. To antique, mix one part black paint with one part water. Brush paint on angel; remove excess with a soft cloth; allow to dry.

4. For halo, form rickrack into a loop; glue ends together at back of angel's head.

5. Cut 1½", 2", and 2½" lengths from braid. Glue one end of each length to the back of one star; glue opposite ends to back of angel's hand.

6. For hanger, fold a 9" length of braid to form a loop; glue ends to back of ornament.

WREATH IN A WINK

It's a snap to make this terrific wreath ornament, and the children can help make it! Simply remove the bottom from an old tart pan and lightly sponge paint the fluted ring. The round opening in the middle is perfect for displaying a favorite photo. For a festive finishing touch, glue buttons and a bow to the front of the wreath.

TART PAN WREATH

You will need a 4⅝" dia. tart pan with removable fluted rim, green acrylic paint, natural sponge piece, hot glue gun, five small red buttons, photograph, cardboard, a 9" length of clear nylon thread, and a 1½" x 18" torn flannel strip.

1. Remove fluted rim from pan. Referring to *Painting Basics*, page 124, lightly Sponge Paint outside of rim green; allow to dry. Glue buttons to rim.

2. Using pan bottom as a pattern, cut circles from cardboard and photograph. Insert photograph, cardboard, then pan bottom into rim to form wreath; glue in place.

3. For hanger, knot ends of nylon thread together to form a loop; glue knot to top of ornament. Tie flannel strip into a bow; trim ends. Glue bow to front of ornament over knot of hanger.

PINT-SIZE COTTAGE

Created by covering a pint-size carton with felt and trims, this little cottage looks good enough to eat!

GINGERBREAD HOUSE

You will need a pint-size milk carton, brown felt, hot glue gun, 3½" x 5½" piece of white cardboard, needle, clear nylon thread, textured glitter snow medium, 1" length of 2"w ribbon, scraps of assorted lace trims, two 2" long plastic candy canes, nine white thumbtacks, red fine-point permanent marker, and a paper doily with a small round motif.

1. Cut away top of carton, leaving triangles at front and back.

2. Draw around bottom of carton on felt; cut out ½" outside drawn line. Center felt on bottom of carton and glue in place, trimming at corners and folding excess to sides. Referring to Fig. 1, draw around all four sides of carton on felt to make one continuous piece to cover sides; cut out. Wrap felt piece around carton and glue in place.

Fig. 1

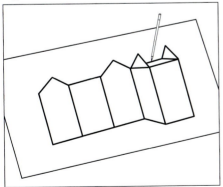

3. To form roof, lightly score across center of cardboard piece; fold in half to form crease.

4. For hanger, use needle to thread the center of a 9" length of nylon thread through center of roof; knot thread ends under roof. Glue roof to carton.

5. Follow manufacturer's instructions to apply snow to top of roof; allow to dry.

6. Glue ribbon to front of carton for door. Glue lengths of lace trims to roof edges, corners, along bottom edges of carton, and to top of door. Glue candy canes to door.

7. Use marker to draw swirls on thumbtacks for peppermint candies; tack to roof and front of carton. Cut round motif from doily; glue to carton front.

SCRAPPY STARS

*D*on't waste those scraps
of holiday fabric and pretty trim!
Use them to create one-of-a-kind
ornaments instead. These scrappy
stars add an elegant touch to gifts,
or you can hang them on the tree.

APPLIQUÉD STARS

For each ornament, you will need paper-
backed fusible web, scraps of assorted
fabrics for appliqués, poster board, 1/8"w
flat gold braid, 3/8"w flat gold trim, eight
6mm gold beads, 3/4" dia. gold shank
button, pliers, and a hot glue gun.

1. Using patterns, page 121, follow
Making Appliqués, page 124, to make
two large star point and six small star
point appliqués from fabrics.

2. Referring to Placement Diagram,
page 121, arrange appliqués on poster
board to form star; fuse in place and cut
out.

3. Glue lengths of braid over raw edges
between star points; glue trim along
outside edges of star.

4. Glue one bead at end of each star
point. Use pliers to remove shank from
button; glue button to center of star.

5. For hanger, fold a 6" length of braid to
form a loop; glue ends to back of
ornament.

SNOW ANGELS

To herald the holidays, craft a host of heavenly snowmen! The cheery snow-cherubs are fashioned from foam trays and corrugated cardboard. As package trims or gifts in themselves, they make great offerings for friends and neighbors!

SNOW ANGELS

You will need tracing paper, foam food tray, corrugated craft cardboard, white and tan acrylic paint, crackling medium, foam brushes, orange and black dimensional paint, hot glue gun, two large white buttons for halos, five small black buttons, six small twigs, and two 3" lengths of white floral wire.

1. Trace patterns, page 105, onto tracing paper; cut out. Using patterns, cut large and small snowmen from tray and large and small wings from cardboard.

2. Following crackling medium manufacturer's instructions and using tan for basecoat and white for top coat, paint snowmen.

3. Use dimensional paint to paint eyes, mouth, and nose on each snowman.

4. Glue black buttons to snowmen.

5. For arms, glue one twig to each side of each snowman. Glue wings to back of each snowman.

6. For halos, cut 1" lengths from remaining twigs. Glue a white button to one end of each twig; glue opposite end of twig to snowman head.

7. For each hanger, twist ends of one wire length together to form a loop; glue to back of ornament.

Children and grown-ups alike will enjoy these sweet inspirations! No one would ever guess that they're all made from items that had been destined for the trash can, such as plastic foam food trays, bottle caps, and plastic lids.

PEPPERMINT ICICLE

You will need three caps from plastic pill bottles; white and red acrylic paint; paintbrushes; clear cellophane; hot glue gun; white, red, and green curling ribbon; and a 9" length of clear nylon thread.

1. For candy pieces, paint caps white; allow to dry. Paint red swirls on each cap; allow to dry. Center each candy piece on a 5" square of cellophane. Twist ends of cellophane to seal.

2. To make ornament, glue ends of candy wrappers together. Place 9" lengths of white, red, and green ribbon together; tie around cellophane between candy pieces. Curl ribbon ends.

3. For hanger, knot ends of nylon thread together; glue knot to back of one end of ornament.

LOLLIPOP

You will need 1 yd. each of white and red 1/4" dia. twisted cord; plastic lid from a snack food container; hot glue gun; lollipop stick; clear cellophane; clear tape; white, red, and green curling ribbon; and a 9" length of clear nylon thread.

1. Placing white and red cords together and beginning at center of lid, arrange cords on lid in a swirl pattern and glue in place.

2. Glue lollipop stick to back of lid.

3. Wrap lollipop with an 11" square of cellophane. Twist cellophane around stick; tape in place. Place 9" lengths of white, red, and green ribbon together; tie around stick, covering tape. Curl ribbon ends.

4. For hanger, knot ends of nylon thread together; glue knot to back of ornament.

GINGERBREAD MAN

You will need a yellow foam food tray; glossy wood tone spray; tracing paper; craft knife; white, pink, red, and black dimensional paint; hot glue gun; lollipop stick; clear cellophane; clear tape; white, red, and green curling ribbon; and a 9" length of clear nylon thread.

1. Trace pattern, page 120, onto tracing paper; cut out. Using pattern and craft knife, cut gingerbread man from foam tray.

2. Lightly spray gingerbread man with wood tone spray; allow to dry.

3. Use dimensional paint to add details to gingerbread man; allow to dry.

4. Glue lollipop stick to back of gingerbread man.

5. Wrap gingerbread man with a 13" square of cellophane. Twist cellophane around stick; tape in place. Place 9" lengths of white, red, and green ribbon together; tie around stick, covering tape. Curl ribbon ends.

6. For hanger, knot ends of nylon thread together; glue knot to back of ornament.

A Touch of Elegance

*D*reaming of an elegant celebration? We can help you create gleaming baubles and brilliant decorations that look like you spent a fortune! No one but you needs to know how much money you saved by hand-crafting these collectible treasures. For example, thread beautiful beads onto lengths of wire to create glittering icicles or shining stars. Surround photocopies of Victorian-style artwork with ribbons and greenery for enchanting cherubs, or create one-of-a-kind ornaments by decorating glass balls with glitter and paint. Turn the page for more grand ideas!

*P*olish up your Yuletide spirit with this crazy-patch trim! A collage of fabrics is arranged to create the festive ornament, which bears a joyous beaded message.

CRAZY-PATCH ORNAMENT

You will need tracing paper, stylus, transfer paper, scraps of assorted fabrics, 4¹/₂" x 6" piece of muslin, sewing thread, items for embellishment (we used a crocheted doily scrap, embroidery floss, and assorted beads), beading thread, beading needle, seed beads for "Joy," batting, poster board, hot glue gun, fabric-covered piping, ¹/₄"w satin ribbon, and two skeins of embroidery floss for tassel.

1. Trace patterns, page 111, onto tracing paper; cut out. Use stylus and transfer paper to transfer "Joy" to a fabric scrap. Leaving at least ¹/₂" outside design, trim fabric to make a five-sided piece (Fig. 1). Center five-sided piece right side up on muslin piece.

Fig. 1

3. Matching right sides and one straight edge, place a second fabric piece on five-sided piece. Stitch through all layers ¹/₄" from matched edges (Fig. 2). Flip second piece right side up and press (Fig. 3).

Fig. 2   **Fig. 3**

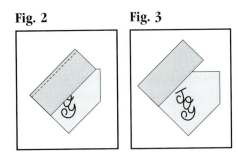

4. (*Note*: Match raw edge of doily scrap to raw edge of one fabric piece and enclose in stitching.) Referring to Figs. 4 and 5, continue to add pieces, stitching, flipping, and pressing, until pieced fabric covers muslin.

Fig. 4   **Fig. 5**

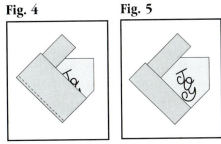

5. Draw around oval pattern on right side of pieced fabric. Referring to *Embroidery Stitches*, page 125, and using three strands of floss, embellish seamlines within drawn oval with desired stitches. Use beading thread and needle and refer to Attaching Beads, page 126, Stitch to stitch "Joy" with seed beads and to add other beads as desired.

6. Cut out embellished oval ¹/₂" outside drawn line. Cut a piece of fabric for backing same size as embellished oval. Using tracing paper oval pattern, cut a piece of batting and two pieces of poster board.

7. Glue batting oval to one poster board oval; center oval batting side down on wrong side of pieced oval. Clip edges of fabric to within ¹/₈" from drawn oval; fold over edges of poster board and glue in place.

8. Beginning and ending at bottom of oval, glue flange of piping around wrong side of pieced oval, trimming to fit.

9. For hanger, fold an 8" length of ribbon to form a loop and glue ends to wrong side of pieced oval.

10. For tassel, cut loops at ends of each skein of embroidery floss; remove labels and place skeins together. Tie a 6" length of floss around center of bundle; fold bundle in half. Wrap additional floss 10 times around tassel approx. ⁷/₈" from top; knot and trim ends. Trim ends of tassel even. Glue tassel hanger to wrong side of pieced oval.

11. Center remaining poster board oval on wrong side of backing fabric oval. Clip edges of fabric close to poster board; fold over edges of poster board and glue in place. Matching wrong sides, glue backing oval to pieced oval.

BAROQUE BEAUTY

*B*ring baroque style to your holiday decor with this ornate trim! It's unbelievably easy to make using decorative metallic braid. Make several to give as last-minute gifts, too.

TASSELED ORNAMENT

You will need a 3" dia. plastic foam ball, sequin pins, assorted colors of Kreinik Metallics Balger® heavy braid, 3½" square of cardboard, liquid fabric stiffener, and a hot glue gun.

1. To cover ball, pin one end of braid to top of ball. Covering ends of braid by wrapping over them, wrap braid around ball, using pins to secure and changing colors of braid as desired until ball is covered.

2. For tassel, wrap several colors of braid around cardboard square 40 to 50 times. Use a length of braid to tightly knot lengths together at one end of cardboard; trim ends close to knot. Cut braid along opposite end of cardboard. Tightly knot a length of braid around tassel ½" from top; trim ends close to knot.

3. To straighten braid, dip tassel in fabric stiffener; remove excess with a paper towel and allow tassel to dry.

4. Glue tassel to bottom of ball, using pins if necessary to secure.

5. For hanger, cut three 12" lengths of braid. Braid lengths together; knot ends of braid together to form a loop. Glue to top of ball. Wrap an additional length of braid around base of hanger, securing with glue and pins as needed.

EXQUISITE ANGELS

*C*lothed in nature's finery, these Victorian adornments will add a charming touch to your evergreen! The delicate cherub faces are copied from postcard art, and leaves and ribbon are glued on for a fanciful touch. For an elegant ending, crown the angels with berry-stem halos.

WOODLAND CHERUBS

For each ornament, you will need a cherub motif cut from giftwrap or a Christmas card; poster board; spray adhesive; a 6" length of 3"w organdy wired ribbon; hot glue gun; a 14" length of 5/8"w wired ribbon; metallic gold acrylic paint; paintbrush; artificial leaves and berries; 5/8"w star sequin; an 8" length of green floral wire; and artificial textured snow.

1. Use spray adhesive to adhere motif to poster board. Cut out cherub face.

2. Bringing wired edges together at bottom, fold organdy ribbon in half lengthwise. Gathering to fit, arrange ribbon along bottom edge of cherub cutout; glue in place. Tie 5/8"w ribbon into a bow; trim ends. Glue bow to organdy ribbon.

3. Glue stem ends of leaves to back of cherub. Trimming to fit, glue small stems of berries behind bow and to cherub hair for halo. Glue sequin to halo.

4. Lightly paint snow on berries; allow to dry. Paint gold highlights around edges of cherub and on leaves, berries, sequin, and ribbons; allow to dry.

5. For hanger, bend floral wire into a loop; glue ends to back of ornament.

PRETTY POINSETTIAS

*D*on't toss out those holiday-print fabric scraps — use them to fashion festive ornaments like these! To make the elegant balls, simply decoupage a print fabric poinsettia motif (or any motif you like) onto white glass ornaments and add details using a gold paint pen.

CHRISTMAS MOTIF ORNAMENTS

For each ornament, you will need a foam brush, decoupage glue, motif cut from Christmas fabric, white glass ornament, gold paint pen, and a 20" length of ¹/₈"w silk ribbon.

Place ornament on a cup while working. Allow glue and paint to dry after each application.

1. Use foam brush and decoupage glue to adhere fabric motif to ornament.

2. Use gold paint pen to draw details on motif and designs on ornament.

3. Thread ribbon through ornament hanger. Leaving a loop for hanging, tie ribbon into a bow.

STYLISH GREETING

Embossed with a holiday message, this velvety door pillow will greet your guests in style! The fashionable accent, finished with gold fringe, is simple to sew by hand or machine. The greeting is pressed into the fabric using a rubber stamp and then accented with paint.

EMBOSSED VELVET PILLOW

You will need a 7¹/₂" x 9¹/₂" piece of 100% rayon velvet, "Merry Christmas" rubber stamp (ours measures 2⁵/₈" x 3⁵/₈"), chalk, water misting bottle, iron, gold glitter dimensional paint, polyester fiberfill, clear nylon thread, two 5¹/₂" lengths of 1"w gold fringe trim, 10¹/₂" length of velvet cord, sprig of artificial holly, hot glue gun, and two 12mm gold jingle bells.

Use a ¹/₄" seam allowance and nylon thread for all sewing.

1. Place velvet piece wrong side up on a flat surface with short edges at top and bottom; center rubber stamp design side down on velvet. Use chalk to mark stamp placement. Remove stamp and place design side up under velvet, aligning with placement marks.

2. To emboss design on velvet, lightly mist velvet with water. Using a hot, dry iron, press velvet onto rubber stamp for 10 to 15 seconds without moving iron. Allow to cool.

3. Paint inside embossed lines; allow to dry.

4. Matching right sides and short edges and leaving an opening for turning, sew short edges together to form a tube. Flatten tube with seam at center back. Sew ends closed; turn right side out. Lightly

stuff pillow with fiberfill; stitch opening closed.

5. Turning raw ends under ¹/₄", sew one length of fringe trim along each end on front of pillow.

6. Turning cord ends under ¹/₄", tack ends of cord to top back corners of pillow for hanger.

7. Remove leaves and berries from pick; glue to center of hanger. Glue bells to hanger.

Crafted from brass wire, faux jewels, and a scrap of tulle, this heavenly adornment lends an artistic touch to your decor. It's easy to coil the wire into shape, and you can make an angel chorus…with no two alike!

DAINTY WIRE ANGEL

You will need 2", 24", and 32" lengths of 20-gauge brass wire; needle nose pliers; five 6mm faceted crystal beads; one 12mm pearl bead; two 6mm round gold washer beads; jewel glue; a 3" x 12" piece of white tulle; and a 9" length of clear nylon thread.

Allow jewel glue to dry after each application.

1. For halo, thread one crystal bead onto 32" wire length. Use pliers to form a 5/8" dia. loop 1/2" from end of wire. With bead on loop; twist wire end to secure.

2. For head and collar, thread pearl bead, then washer beads onto wire below halo. Bend wire to hold beads in place.

3. For body, form another 5/8" dia. loop below collar. Continue forming slightly larger loops for a 3 1/2"h body with a total of six loops. Thread remaining crystal beads onto wire; form wire end into a flat coil. Position beads on wire as desired and glue in place.

4. Referring to photo, shape 24" wire length to form wings. Twist ends of wire together at center. Use 2" wire length to attach wings to angel between pearl and washer beads; glue to secure.

5. To gather tulle, work a Running Stitch, page 126, along one long edge. Pull thread to gather; knot thread. Use thread ends to tie skirt in place on angel at neck; glue to secure. Trim thread ends.

6. For hanger, knot ends of nylon thread together; glue knot to back of ornament.

DAZZLING DISPLAY

Looking for a new way to showcase your tree adornments? Decorated with swirls of gold and acrylic jewels, simple glass ball ornaments make a dazzling tabletop arrangement when displayed in a stylized goblet.

GILDED GLASS BALLS

For each ornament, you will need Gallery Glass® gold liquid leading, silicone household glue, and a 9" length of clear nylon thread.

For large ornament, you will also need a 4" dia. glass ball ornament, Gallery Glass® ruby red glass paint, paintbrush, opalescent and green glass stones, and 1 yd. of 2½"w sheer wired ribbon.

For small ornament, you will also need a 3" dia. glass ball ornament, and 7mm red and 9mm green acrylic jewels.

Place each ornament on a cup while working. Allow leading, paint, and glue to dry after each application.

1. Use gold leading to paint swirls on each ornament.

2. For large ornament, paint back of each opalescent stone red.

3. Glue jewels or stones to ornament.

4. For large ornament, tie ribbon into a bow around ornament hanger; trim ends.

5. For each hanger, thread nylon thread through ornament hanger; knot ends together.

REGAL TREASURES

It's easy to transform plain glass ornaments into baubles fit for royalty! Simply embellish them with iridescent glitter paint and rich gold accents to create regal treasures for your holiday display.

GLITTER ORNAMENTS

For each ornament, you will need a gold paint pen, red glass ball ornament, small paintbrush, and gold iridescent glitter paint.

Place ornament on a cup while working. Allow paint to dry after each application.

1. Use paint pen to draw a squiggly line around center of ornament.

2. Use brush and glitter paint to paint ornament below line.

GILDED GRANDEUR

A Victorian cone and gleaming ball make grand ornaments for trimming the tree. Exquisitely embellished with gold braid and fanciful wrapping paper, the cone is not just beautiful on the outside, but it also holds a delicate bouquet of roses, greenery, and baby's breath. Equally stunning, the bedazzling ball features a distinctive drapery of seed beads and a festive ribbon.

BEDAZZLING ORNAMENT

You will need liquid fray preventative; an 8" length of 1 1/2"w sheer ribbon; beading needle; beading thread; gold, red, and green seed beads; gold bugle beads; hot glue gun; 2 1/2" dia. gold ball ornament; 3 1/2" of 1/2"w gold braid; 14" of 7/8"w gold mesh wired ribbon; and a 9" length of clear nylon thread.

1. Apply fray preventative to ends of sheer ribbon; allow to dry.

2. For beaded scallop on ribbon, thread beading needle with beading thread; take a small stitch at edge near one end of ribbon. Thread two gold, two green, two red, and two gold seed beads onto needle. Take a small stitch on ribbon edge 3/8" from first stitch. Repeat to make two more scallops.

3. For drop, thread one gold seed bead, one red seed bead, one gold bugle bead, and one green seed bead onto needle. Run needle back through bugle bead, then add one red and one gold seed bead (Fig. 1). Take a small stitch on ribbon edge.

Fig. 1

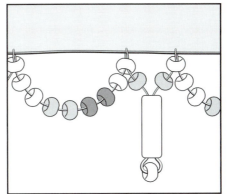

4. Repeat Steps 2 and 3 along remainder of ribbon edge. Knot and trim thread.

5. Work a Running Stitch, page 126, along opposite ribbon edge. Pull thread to gather ribbon edge to fit around top of ornament. Knot and trim thread. Tack ends of beaded ribbon edge together.

6. Glue 1/2"w braid around ornament top, covering gathered ribbon edge.

7. Thread gold ribbon through hanging loop on ornament and tie into a bow; trim ends.

8. For hanger, thread nylon thread through hanging loop; knot thread ends together.

VICTORIAN CONE

You will need tracing paper; transfer paper; stylus; 6 1/2" squares of poster board and gold gift wrap; spray adhesive; hot glue gun; a 10" length of 1/4"w gold braid; tissue paper; dried small roses, baby's breath, and greenery; 3/4 yd. of 3/16"w gold ribbon; and a gold charm.

1. Trace cone pattern, page 122, onto tracing paper. Use transfer paper to transfer pattern to poster board. Cut shape from poster board. Use stylus to score each transferred dashed line.

2. Spray unscored side of poster board shape with adhesive. Center gift wrap over poster board and smooth in place; trim edges even with edges of poster board.

3. To form cone, bend poster board on each scored line; overlap sections at each end and glue in place.

4. Glue braid around top edge of cone, trimming to fit.

5. Place crumpled tissue paper inside cone. Arrange roses, baby's breath, and greenery in cone opening and glue in place.

6. For handle, glue ends of a 7" length of ribbon to opposite sides of cone. Tie two 10" ribbon lengths into bows; trim ends. Glue one bow over each end of handle.

7. Glue charm to cone.

FROSTED ELEGANCE

For an elegant look, adorn your tree with shimmery strawberry ornaments! They're a cinch to make: simply take a strawberry pick and brush the greenery with gold paint to give it a cheery glow; then glue iridescent seed beads to the berries. For a festive finish, top with a beautiful bow.

FROSTED STRAWBERRY DECORATION
You will need metallic gold acrylic paint, small paintbrush, artificial strawberry pick with greenery, craft glue, iridescent seed beads, a 16" length of 2½"w wired ribbon, a 9" length of gold cord, and a hot glue gun.

1. Lightly paint edges of leaves and other greenery gold; allow to dry.

2. Spread a thin layer of craft glue on each berry; dip into beads and allow to dry.

3. Tie ribbon into a bow around pick; trim ends.

4. For hanger, fold cord to form a loop; hot glue cord ends to back of stem.

OLDE WORLD SANTA

Tucked among the branches of an evergreen or displayed on the wall, this handsome picture adds nostalgia to your celebration. The dimensional look is created by layering cutouts from identical greeting cards.

THREE-DIMENSIONAL DECORATION
You will need card stock, cardboard, five identical Christmas cards, frame with opening larger than cards, craft glue, clear silicone adhesive, and a gold paint pen.

1. Cut card stock and cardboard to fit frame opening. Use craft glue to glue card stock to cardboard; allow to dry.

2. Cut fronts from Christmas cards. Center one card front on prepared card stock and glue in place. Cut desired shapes from remaining cards.

3. (*Note:* Allow adhesive to become tacky before adhering shapes.) Beginning with largest shapes first, use silicone to glue shapes to front of card; allow to dry.

4. Use gold pen to outline edges of card cutouts and add details as desired.

5. Mount card in frame.

SEASIDE TREASURES

*B*ring back memories of summer days at the seaside with these nautical trims. Simply dress up shells and starfish with shimmering floral spray, pretty beads, and golden wire accents.

BEADED STARFISH

You will need a starfish, Floralife® Pearl Shimmer Spray, 4mm iridescent pearl string beads, 2.5mm clear iridescent string beads, hot glue gun, craft glue, small shell for center, assorted iridescent seed beads, a 10" length of 20-gauge gold wire, and a 6" length of clear nylon thread.

1. Spray starfish with Pearl Shimmer; allow to dry.

2. Wrapping from front to back, hot glue one length of 4mm beads into each space between starfish arms.

3. Hot glue a length of 2.5mm string beads along center of each arm.

94

4. Hot glue small shell to center of starfish.

5. Using craft glue, glue additional 4mm beads and seed beads to center of star around shell; allow to dry. Hot glue one bead inside shell.

6. Wrap center of gold wire around end of one starfish arm; twist once to hold. Form each end of wire into a flat coil.

7. For hanger, thread nylon thread through back of gold wire; knot ends. Secure at back of wire with hot glue.

SINGLE AUGER SEASHELL ORNAMENT

You will need an auger seashell, Floralife® Pearl Shimmer spray, 20-gauge gold wire, wire cutters, hot glue gun, 4mm iridescent pearl string beads, assorted iridescent seed beads, craft glue, and a 9" length of clear nylon thread.

1. Spray shell with Pearl Shimmer; allow to dry.

2. Bend one end of wire into a small hook shape; hook to opening of shell. Hot glue hook to secure. Tightly wrap wire around shell, following indentation. At tip of shell, leave 2½" of wire; cut off excess. Form end of wire into a small flat coil.

3. Form three additional wire lengths into tight flat coils; hot glue wire ends inside shell opening.

4. Hot glue string pearls around shell opening. Use craft glue to glue seed beads around string beads.

5. Knot ends of nylon thread together to form loop; glue knot to back of ornament.

DOUBLE AUGER SEASHELL ORNAMENT

You will need hot glue gun, two auger seashells, Floralife® Pearl Shimmer spray, 4mm iridescent pearl string beads, 20-gauge gold wire, wire cutters, craft glue, assorted iridescent seed beads, and a 9" length of clear nylon thread.

1. Hot glue shells together at openings.

2. Spray shells with Pearl Shimmer; allow to dry.

3. Wrap and hot glue string pearls around "seam" between shells. Use craft glue to glue seed beads around pearls; allow to dry.

4. Form one end of wire into a ³/₈" flat coil. Beginning at one end, tightly wrap wire around shells, following indentations. At opposite end of ornament, leave 2½" of wire; cut off excess. Form end of wire into a small flat coil.

5. For hanger, knot ends of nylon thread together to form loop; glue knot to back of ornament.

AUGER SEASHELL STAR ORNAMENT

You will need five auger seashells, a ³/₄" dia. wooden star cutout, Floralife® Pearl Shimmer spray, hot glue gun, 4mm iridescent pearl string beads, two small seashells, craft glue, assorted iridescent seed beads, a 6½" length of 20-gauge gold wire, wire cutters, and a 9" length of clear nylon thread.

1. Spray shells with Pearl Shimmer; allow to dry.

2. With star point inside shell opening, hot glue one auger shell over each point of wooden star.

3. Wrapping from front to back, hot glue a length of string pearls into the space between each pair of auger shells.

4. Hot glue small shells to front and back of star.

5. Use craft glue to glue seed beads to front and back of star around small shells; allow to dry.

6. Wrap center of wire around tip of one auger shell; twist to secure. Form each end of gold wire into a small flat coil.

7. For hanger, knot ends of nylon thread together to form loop; glue knot to back of ornament.

SIMPLE ELEGANCE

This beaded beauty is a snap to make! Simply wrap lustrous fabric around a foam ball, gather the edges together, and secure with a rubber band. Then pin seed beads into the ball to form intriguing swirls or other designs. Simple yet elegant!

PIN-BEADED ORNAMENT

You will need 1/8" dia. gold twisted cord, straight pin, 3" dia. foam ball, 18" square of fabric, 7" length of floral wire, liquid fray preventative, 1/2" long gold sequin pins, and silver seed beads.

1. For hanger, knot ends of a 9" length of cord together to form a loop. Using straight pin, pin knot to top of ball.

2. Center ball on wrong side of fabric. Gather edges of fabric around hanger; secure by wrapping tightly with floral wire. Adjust gathers; trim fabric edges and apply fray preventative; allow to dry.

3. Wrap and knot a 9" length of cord over floral wire; knot ends of cord.

4. Picking up a bead with each sequin pin, push pins into ball to form swirl and diamond designs.

SPARKLING SPIRAL

*O*ur spiral spangle makes a
magnificent ornament for the
evergreen. But don't be fooled by
its intricate appearance — the
alluring adornment is actually a
cinch to make! Just thread beads
onto wire and then twist to perfection.
For an exceptionally exquisite look,
fill your tree with these dazzling
decorations!

BEADED SPIRAL

You will need needle-nose pliers, a 9"
length of 28-gauge gold wire, a large
crystal drop, clear glass seed beads, a
16" length of 20-gauge gold wire, silver
mushroom beads, silver washer beads,
and clear faceted beads.

1. For beaded wire with crystal drop,
thread one end of 28-gauge wire through
hole in crystal drop. Use pliers to twist
wire end around itself above drop. Thread
seed beads onto wire. Make a bend in
wire end to secure beads; set aside.

2. For beaded spiral wire, bend one end
of 20-gauge wire into a small loop.
Thread beads onto wire in the following
order: one mushroom, one washer, three
faceted, and one washer. Repeat thirteen
more times.

3. To attach beaded drop wire to
beaded spiral wire, wrap end of drop
wire tightly around beaded wire and
last washer bead.

4. For hanger, form a 1/2" dia. loop in
wire above last washer bead; twist wire
end around 28-gauge wire to secure.

5. Form beaded wire into a spiral
around drop.

STELLAR SENSATION

It's unbelievably easy to make this stellar ornament! Simply form wire into star shapes and thread beads onto each one. For fancy finishing touches, top with a festive bow and hang a glass ball ornament in the center.

BEADED WIRE STAR

You will need a glass bead garland, wire cutters, 19-gauge wire, 3/8"w gold wired ribbon, hot glue gun, gold paint pen, 2" dia. glass ball ornament, and a 10" length of 1/16"w gold braid.

1. Remove beads from garland.

2. Using wire cutters, cut two 20" pieces of wire. Referring to pattern, page 99, form each wire piece into a star shape. Thread beads onto each star shape; twist wire ends together and trim.

3. Place one star shape inside the other and secure at top and bottom with small pieces of wire.

4. Using paint pen, paint "Joy" on ball ornament; allow to dry.

5. Thread braid through hanger on ball ornament; tie around top of stars so that ball hangs inside stars. Knot ends of braid to form hanger loop.

6. Use gold ribbon to tie a triple-loop bow; glue bow to top of stars.

PATTERNS

BEADED WIRE STAR

STAR

HOMEY SANTA

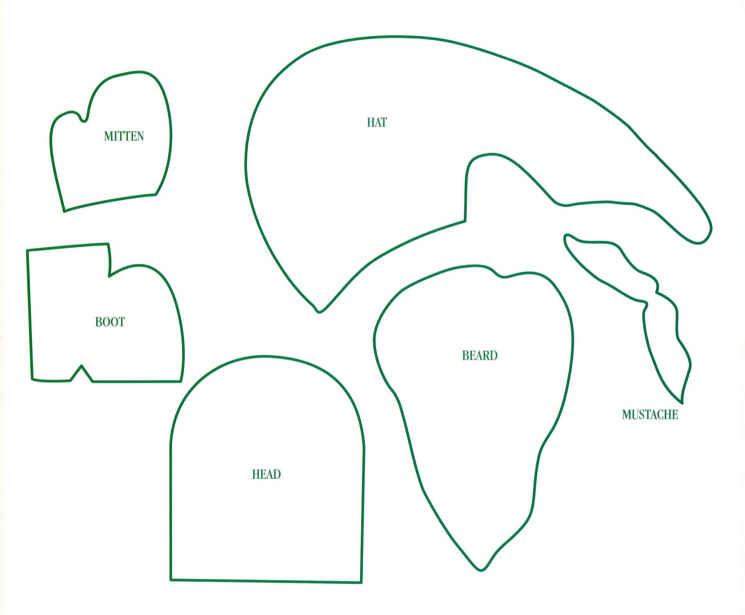

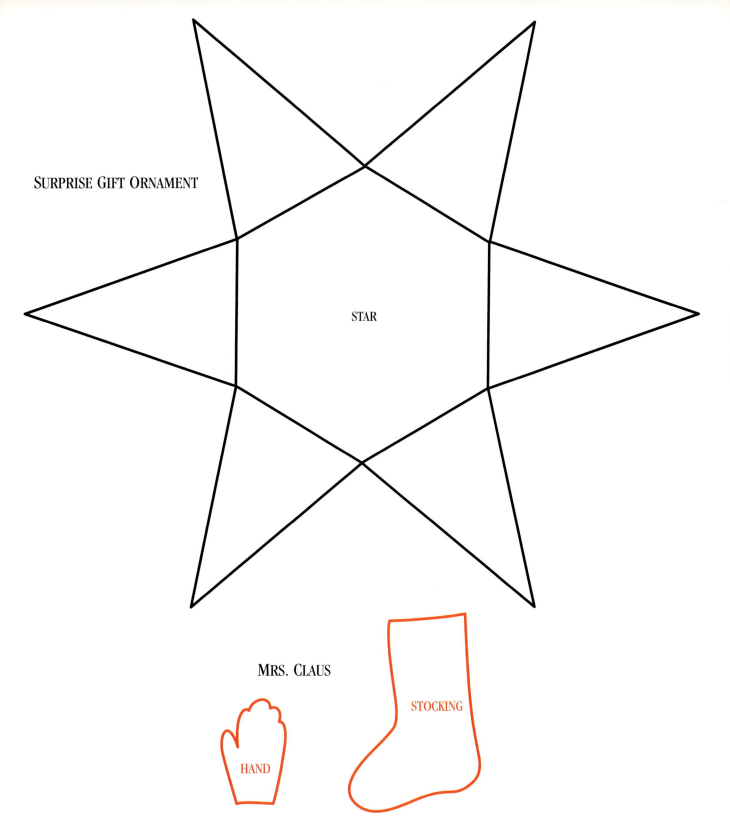

SURPRISE GIFT ORNAMENT

STAR

MRS. CLAUS

HAND

STOCKING

HOMESPUN ORNAMENTS

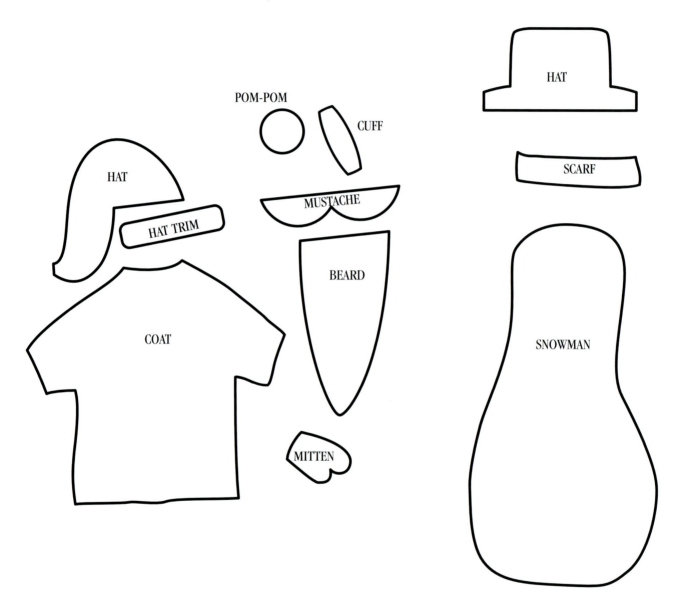

POM-POM

CUFF

HAT

HAT

SCARF

HAT TRIM

MUSTACHE

BEARD

COAT

SNOWMAN

MITTEN

FAUX STAINED-GLASS ORNAMENTS

ANGEL

SMALL STAR

PAINT BRUSH SANTA

LARGE STAR

FELT MOSIAC DOVE

BERRY

LEAF

BEAK

DOVE BODY

Peace

CUFF

STOCKING

FELT STOCKING
ORNAMENTS

TOE

HEEL

STAR

TREE

MOON

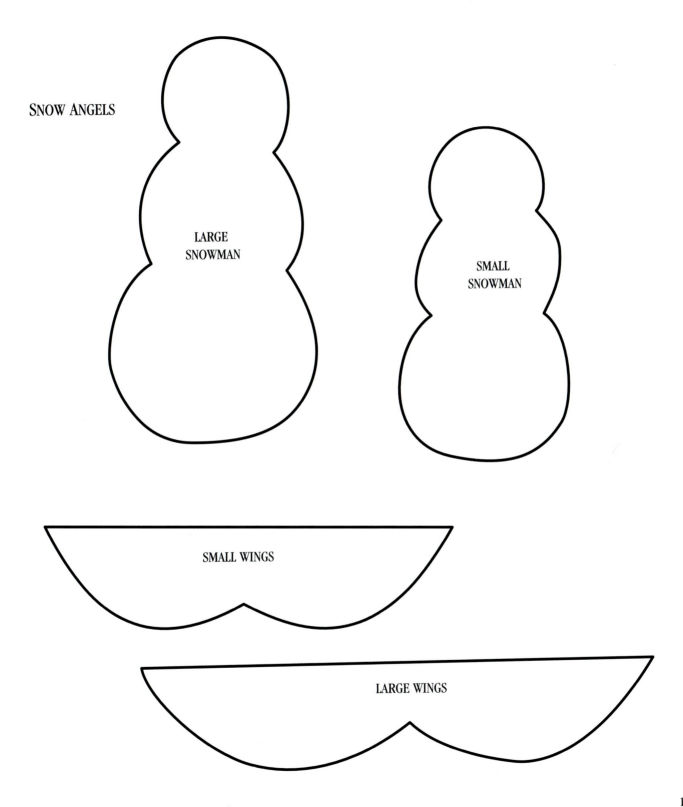

SNOW ANGELS

LARGE
SNOWMAN

SMALL
SNOWMAN

SMALL WINGS

LARGE WINGS

105

PATTERNS (continued)

CHRISTMAS CARDINALS

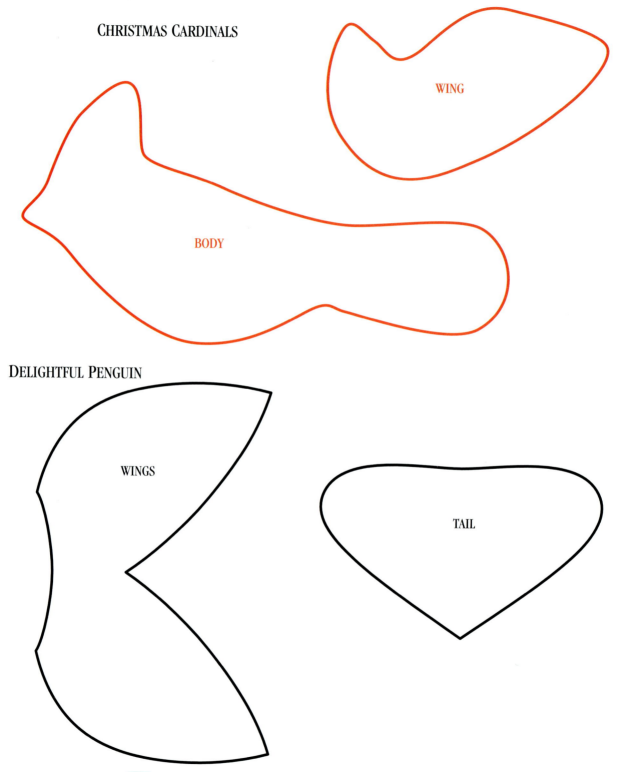

WING

BODY

DELIGHTFUL PENGUIN

WINGS

TAIL

PATTERNS (continued)

GARDEN GLOVE SANTA

BOOT

HEAD

ELVIN THE ELF

HAT

HAT TRIM

HEAD

PHOTO IMAGE SANTA STAR

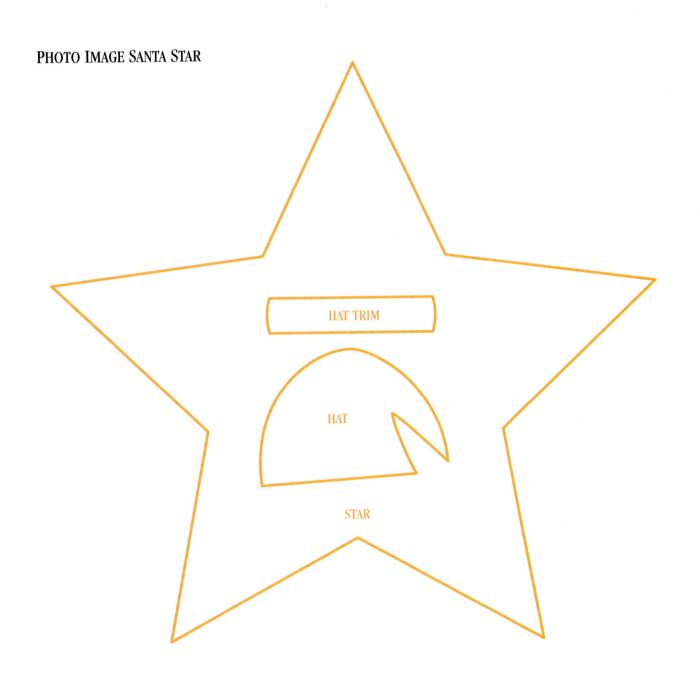

HAT TRIM

HAT

STAR

PATTERNS (continued)

SOCK REINDEER

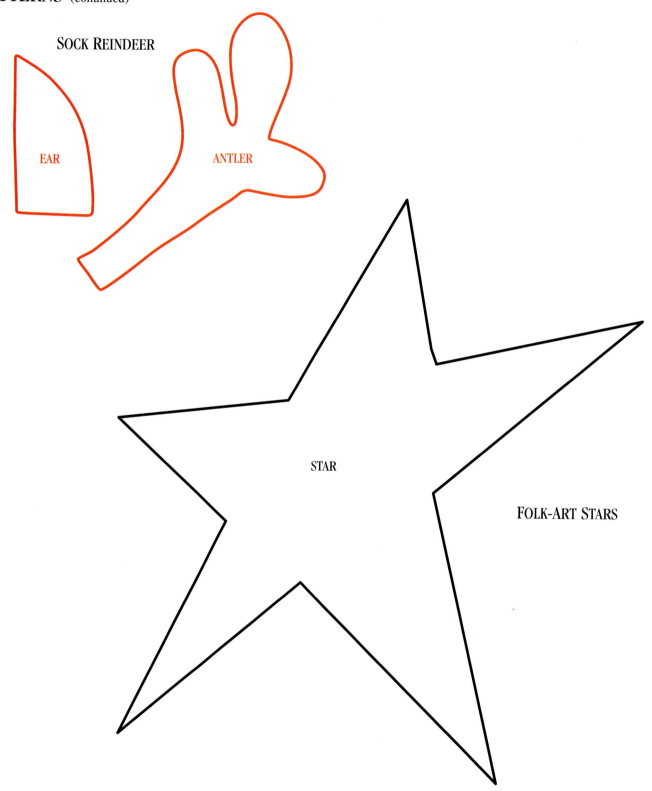

EAR

ANTLER

STAR

FOLK-ART STARS

APPLIQUÉ DOVE

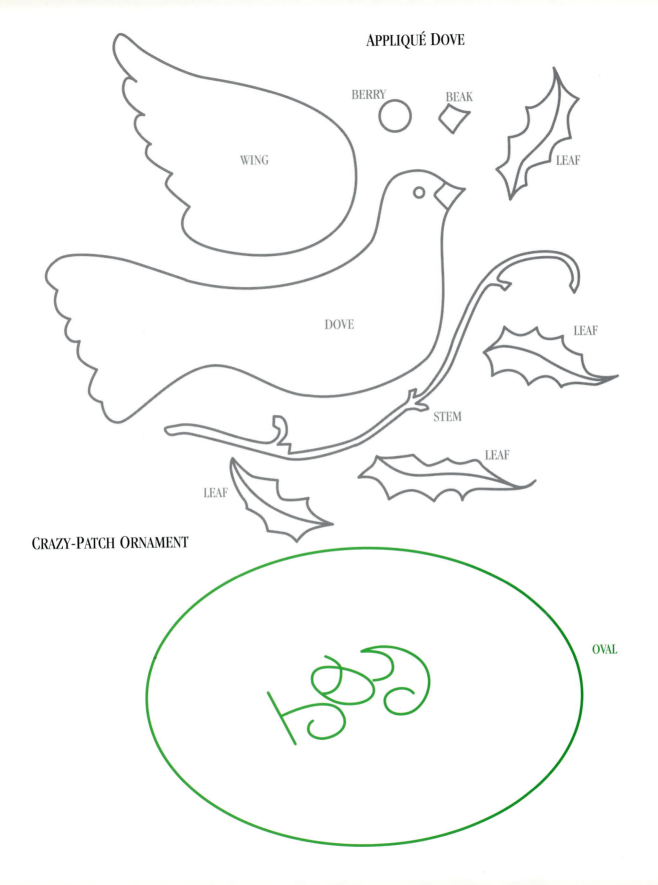

BERRY

BEAK

LEAF

WING

LEAF

DOVE

LEAF

STEM

LEAF

LEAF

CRAZY-PATCH ORNAMENT

OVAL

ANGEL TREE TOPPER

BUTTON ANGELS

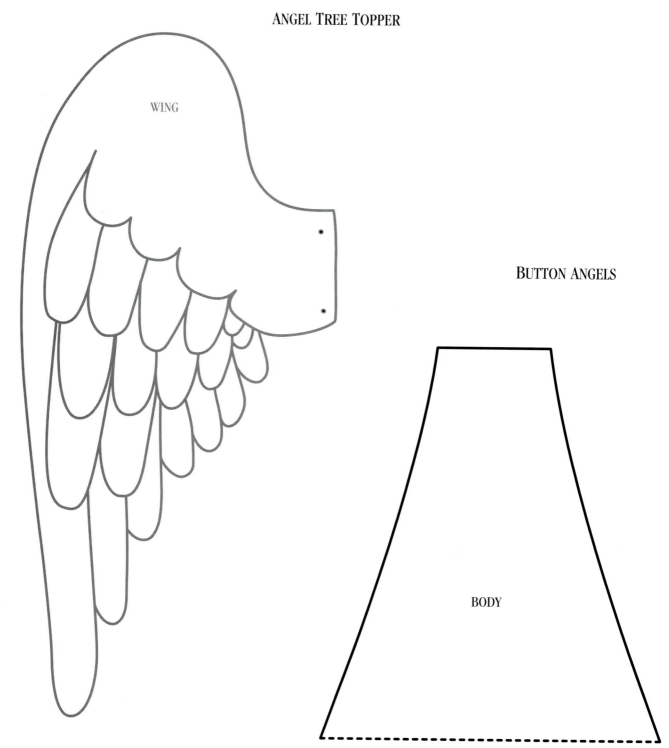

WING

BODY

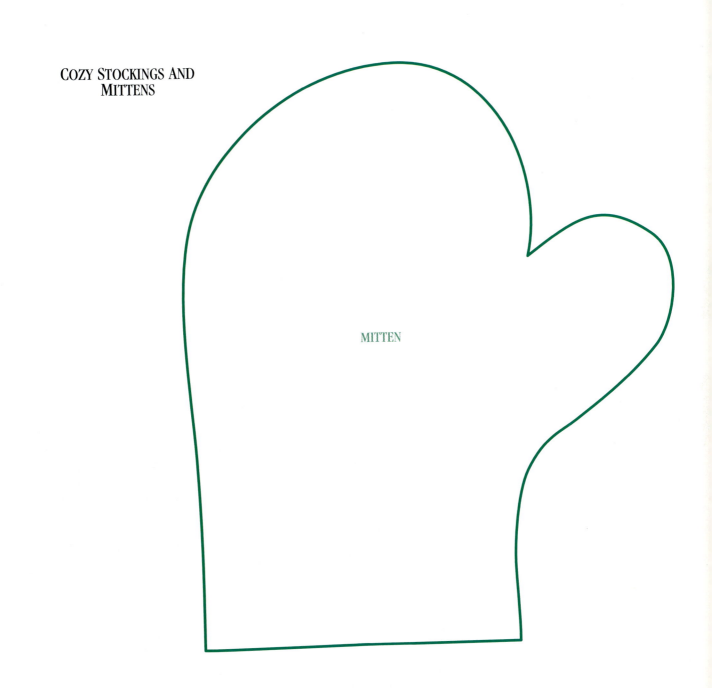

MITTEN

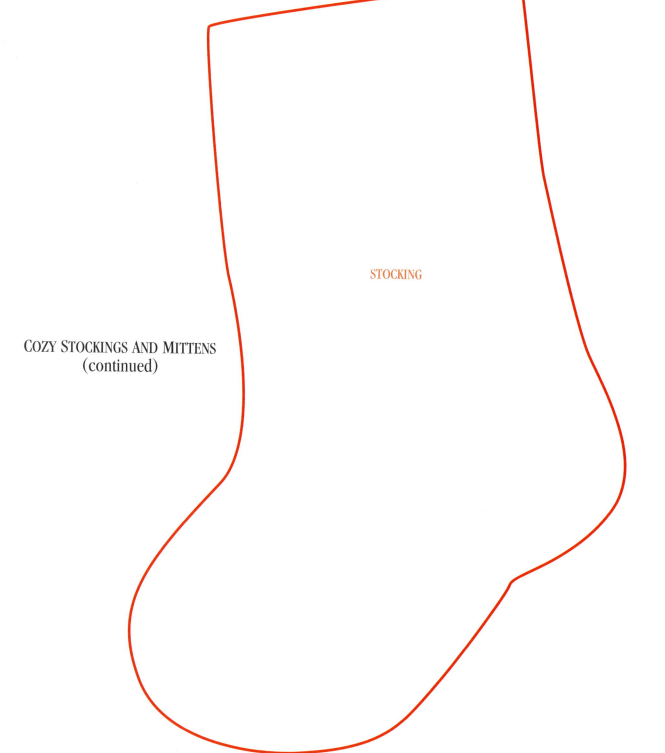

STOCKING

COZY STOCKINGS AND MITTENS
(continued)

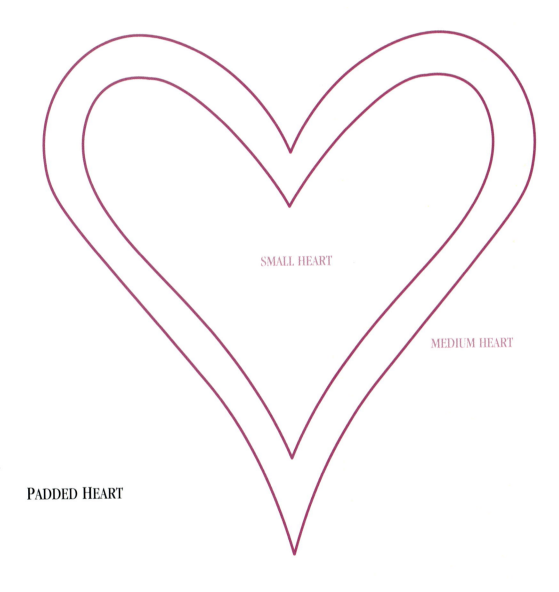

SMALL HEART

MEDIUM HEART

PADDED HEART

MERRY MESSAGE FOR TEACHER

Merry Christmas, Teacher!

NATURAL ORNAMENTS

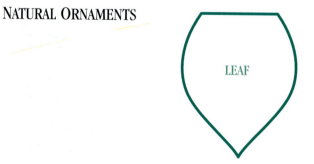

LEAF

FLOCKED ORNAMENTS

SANTA

SHEEP

PATTERNS (continued)

CHRISTMAS MICE

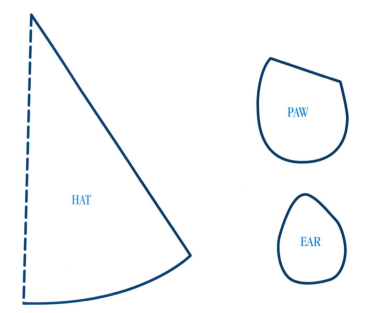

HANDCRAFTED SANTA

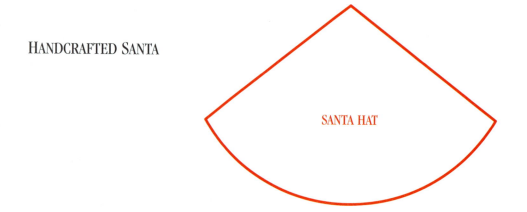

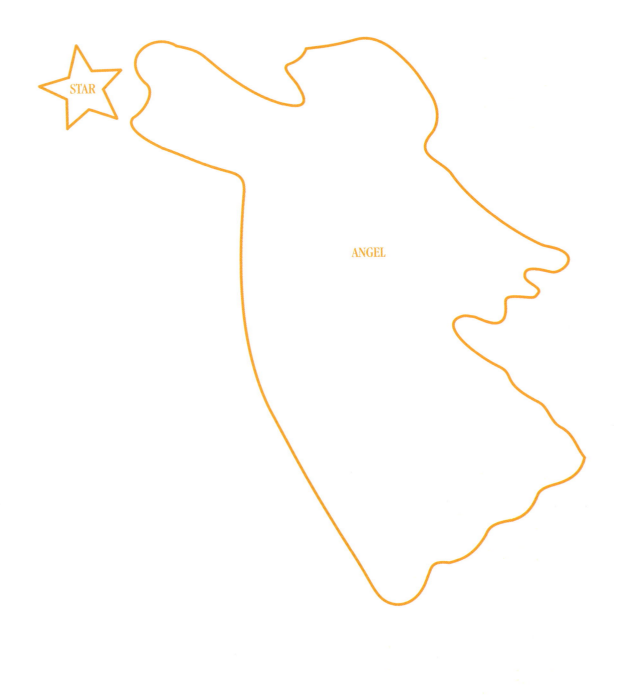

STAR

ANGEL

GINGERBREAD MAN

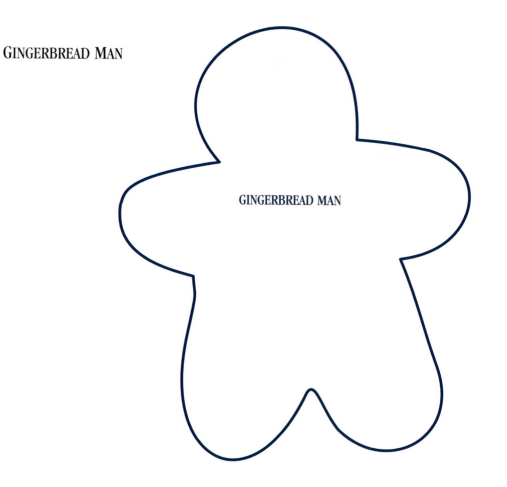

GINGERBREAD MAN

BABY'S FIRST CHRISTMAS

MITTEN

NOSE

APPLIQUÉD STARS

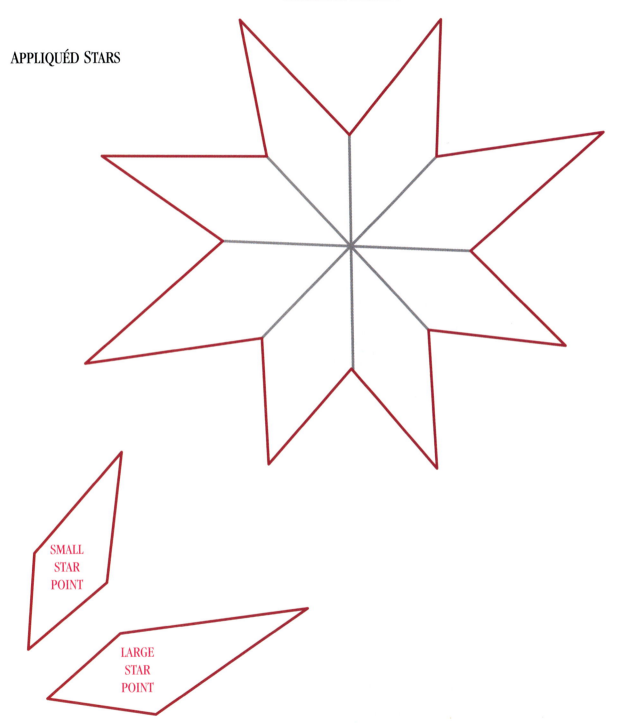

SMALL
STAR
POINT

LARGE
STAR
POINT

PATTERNS (continued)

VICTORIAN CONE

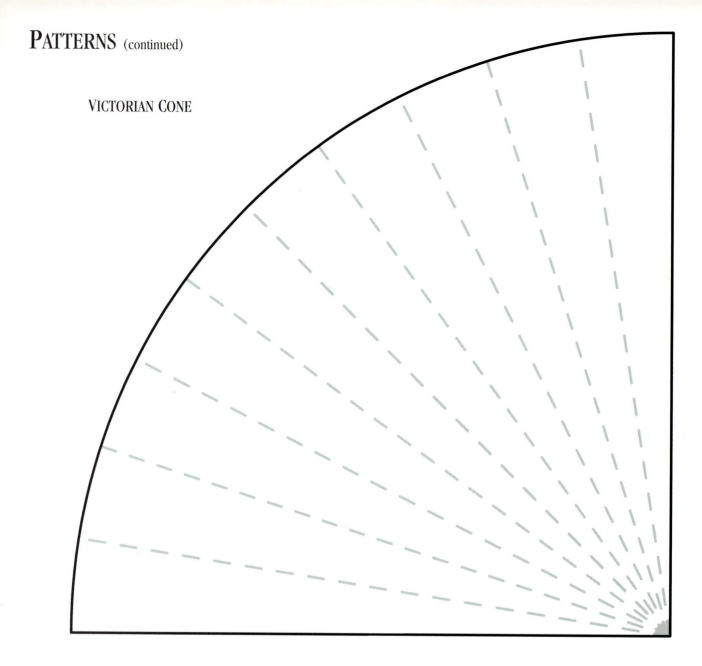

CRUSHED CAN COWBOY

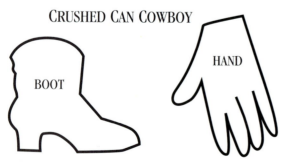

BOOT

HAND

PINT SIZE NUTCRACKER

JACKET

FACE

Beaded Cross Stitch Ornaments

X	DMC	¼X	B'ST	ANC.	COLOR
•	blanc	•		2	white
	310		╱	403	black
✿	311			148	dk blue
∏	312			979	blue
✹	319			218	vy dk green
4	320			215	green
‰	322			978	lt blue
✕	334			977	vy lt blue
5	367			217	dk green
✩	368			214	lt green
◓	433			358	dk brown
V	434	◪		310	brown
▢	435			1046	lt brown
+	436			1045	vy lt brown
8	611			898	taupe
◀	612			832	lt taupe
✤	644			830	beige grey
✳	725			305	dk yellow
T	754			1012	flesh
$	761			1021	lt pink
◉	783			307	gold
▲	814	◪		45	dk maroon
◕	816			1005	lt maroon
▽	822			390	lt beige grey
d	948			1011	lt flesh
•	Mill Hill Bead - 00161				
•	Mill Hill Bead - 00431				
•	Mill Hill Bead - 00148				
•	Mill Hill Bead - 00968				
•	310			403	black Fr. Knot

HEARTY SANTA

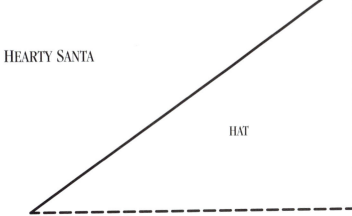

HAT

GENERAL INSTRUCTIONS

MAKING PATTERNS
Dashed line on pattern indicates where traced pattern is to be placed on fold of fabric.

When patterns are stacked or overlapped, place tracing paper over pattern and follow a single colored line to trace pattern. Repeat to trace each pattern separately onto tracing paper.

For a more durable pattern, use translucent vinyl template material instead of tracing paper.

Half-patterns: Fold tracing paper in half. Place fold along dotted line and trace pattern half; turn folded paper over and draw over traced lines on remaining side. Unfold pattern; cut out.

Two-part patterns: Trace one part of pattern onto tracing paper. Match dashed line and arrows of traced part with dashed line and arrows of second part in book and trace second part; cut out.

Transferring a Pattern: Make a tracing paper pattern. Position pattern on project. Place transfer paper coated side down between pattern and project. Use a stylus or ballpoint pen to trace over lines of patterns.

SEWING SHAPES
1. Center pattern on wrong side of one fabric piece and use fabric marking pencil or pen to draw around pattern. DO NOT CUT OUT SHAPE.

2. Place fabric pieces right sides together. Leaving an opening for turning, carefully sew pieces together directly on pencil line.

3. Leaving a $1/4$" seam allowance, cut out shape. Clip seam allowance at curves and corners. Turn shape right side out.

MAKING APPLIQUÉS
To protect your ironing board, cover with muslin. Web material that sticks to iron may be removed with hot iron cleaner, available at fabric and craft stores.

To prevent darker fabrics from showing through, white or light-colored fabrics may need to be lined with fusible interfacing before being fused.

Trace appliqué pattern onto paper side of web. If pattern is a half-pattern or to make a reversed appliqué, make a tracing paper pattern (turn traced pattern over for reversed appliqué) and follow instructions using traced pattern. When making more than one appliqué, leave at least 1" between shapes. Cutting $1/2$" outside drawn shape, cut out web shape. Fuse to wrong side of fabric. Cut out shape along drawn lines. Remove paper backing. Fuse appliqués in place.

STITCHING APPLIQUÉS
Place paper or stabilizer on wrong side of background fabric under fused appliqué. Set machine for a narrow zigzag stitch.

Beginning on a straight edge of appliqué if possible, position project under presser foot so that most of stitching will be on appliqué. Take a stitch in fabric and bring bobbin thread to top. Hold both threads toward you and sew over them for several stitches to secure; clip threads. Stitch over all exposed raw edges of appliqué(s) and along detail lines as indicated in instructions.

When stitching is complete, remove stabilizer. Clip threads close to stitching.

PAINTING BASICS
Painting base coats: A disposable foam plate makes a good palette. Use a medium round brush for large areas and a small round brush for small areas. Do not overload brush. Allowing to dry between coats, apply several thin coats of paint to project.

Transferring a pattern: Trace pattern onto tracing paper. Place transfer paper coated side down between project and traced pattern. Use removable tape to secure pattern to project. Use a pencil to transfer outlines of design to project (press lightly to avoid smudges and heavy lines that are difficult to cover). If necessary, use a soft eraser to remove any smudges.

Sponge painting: Pour a small amount of paint onto a paper plate. Dip dampened sponge piece into paint and remove excess on a paper towel. Use a light stamping motion to apply paint. Reapply paint to sponge as necessary.

Sealing: If an item will be handled frequently or used outdoors, we recommend sealing the item with a clear acrylic sealer. Sealers are available in spray or brush-on form in several finishes. Follow manufacturer's instructions to apply sealer.

Spatter painting: Dip the bristle tips of a toothbrush into paint, blot on paper towel to remove excess, then pull thumb across bristles to spatter paint on project.

Painting with dimensional paint: Turn bottle upside down to fill tip before each use. While painting, clean tip often with a paper towel. If tip becomes clogged, insert a straight pin into opening to unclog.

To paint, touch tip to project. Squeezing and moving bottle steadily, apply paint to project, being careful not to flatten paint line. If painting detail lines, center line of paint over transferred line on project or freehand details as desired.

To correct a mistake, use a paring knife to gently scrape excess paint from project before it dries. Carefully remove stain with non-acetone nail polish remover on a cotton swab. A mistake may also be camouflaged by incorporating it into the design.

MAKING A BOW
Making a multi-loop bow: For first streamer, measure desired length of streamer from one end of ribbon; twist ribbon between fingers. Keeping right side of ribbon facing out, fold ribbon to front to form desired-size loop; gather ribbon between fingers (Fig. 1). Fold ribbon to back to form another loop; gather ribbon between fingers (Fig. 2).

Fig. 1   **Fig. 2**

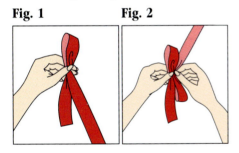

(Note: If a center loop is desired, form half the desired number of loops, then loosely wrap ribbon around thumb and gather ribbon between fingers as shown in Fig. 3; form remaining loop.) Continue to form loops, varying size of loops.

Fig. 3

For remaining streamer, trim ribbon to desired length.

To secure bow, hold gathered loops tightly. Fold a length of floral wire around gathers. Holding wire ends behind bow and gathering loops forward; twist bow to tighten wire. Arrange loops and trim ribbon ends.

EMBROIDERY STITCHES
Preparing floss: If using embroidery floss for a project that will be laundered, soak floss in a mixture of one cup water and one tablespoon vinegar for a few minutes and allow to dry before using to prevent colors from bleeding or fading.

Blanket Stitch: Referring to Fig. 1, bring needle up at 1. Keeping thread below point of needle, go down at 2 and come up at 3. Continue working as shown in Fig. 2.

Fig. 1   **Fig. 2**

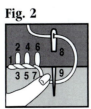

Feather Stitch: Come up at 1. Go down at 2 and come up at three, keeping floss below point of needle (Fig. 3). Alternate stitches from right to left, keeping stitches symmetrical (Fig. 4).

Fig. 3   **Fig. 4**

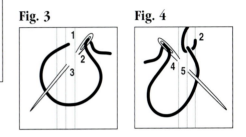

French Knot: Bring needle up at 1. Wrap floss once around needle and insert needle at 2, holding end of floss with non-stitching fingers. Tighten knot, then pull needle through fabric, holding floss until it must be released. For a larger knot, use more strands; wrap only once.

Fig. 5

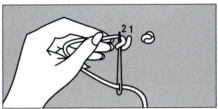

Fly Stitch: Bring needle up at 1; go down at 2 and come up at 3, keeping floss below point of needle. Take needle back down at 4 (Fig. 6).

Fig. 6

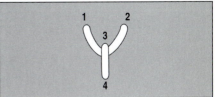

Herringbone Stitch: Bring nedle up at 1; take needle down at 2 and come up at 3 (Fig. 7). Go down at 4 and come up at 5 (Fig. 8). continue working as shown in Fig. 9.

Fig. 7

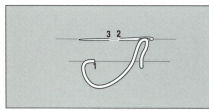

Fig. 8

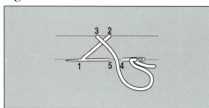

Fig. 9

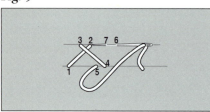

Running Stitch: Referring to Fig. 10, make a series of straight stitches with stitch length equal to the space between stitches.

Fig. 10

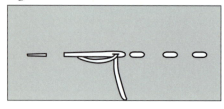

Overcast Stitch: Bring needle up at 1; take thread over edge of fabric and bring needle up at 2. Continue stitching aong edge of fabric (Fig. 11)

Fig.11

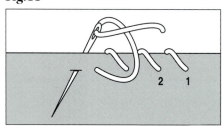

Satin Stitch: Referring to Fig. 12, come up at odd numbers and go down at even numbers with the stitches touching but not overlapping.

Fig. 12

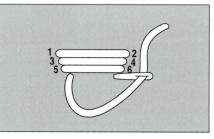

Stem Stitch: Referring to Fig. 13, come up at 1. Keeping thread below stitching line, go down at 2 and come up at 3. Go down at 4 and come up at 5.

Fig. 13

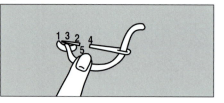

Straight Stitch: Referring to Fig. 14, come up at 1 and go down at 2.

Fig. 14

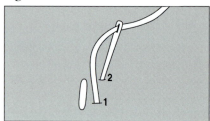

CROSS STITCH

Preparing floss: If your project will be laundered, soak floss in a mixture of one cup water and one tablespoon vinegar for a few minutes and allow to dry before using to prevent colors from bleeding or fading.

Attaching Beads: Refer to chart for bead placement, use two strands of floss and use a fine needle that will pass through bead. Secure floss on back of fabric. Bring needle up where indicated on chart, then run needle through bead and down through fabric. Secure floss on back or move to next bead.

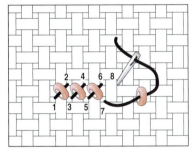

Counted Cross Stitch (X): Work one Cross Stitch to correspond to each colored square in chart. For horizontal rows, work stitches in two journeys.

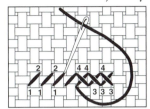

For vertical rows, complete each stitch as shown.

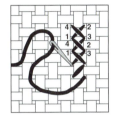

When working over two fabric threads, work Cross Stitch as shown.

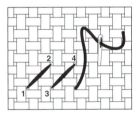

Quarter Stitch (¼ X): Quarter Stitches are shown by triangular shapes of color in chart and color key.

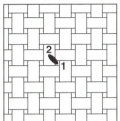

Backstitch (B'ST): For outline detail, Backstitch (shown in chart and color key by black or colored straight lines) should be worked after all Cross Stitch has been completed.

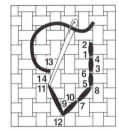

CREDITS

To Wisconsin Technicolor LLC of Pewaukee, Wisconsin, we say *thank you* for the superb color reproduction and excellent pre-press preparation.

We want to especially thank photographers Larry Pennington, Ken West, and Andy Uilkie of Peerless Photography, Little Rock, Arkansas, and Jerry R. Davis of Jerry Davis Photography, Little Rock, Arkansas, for their time, patience, and excellent work.

To the talented people who helped in the creation of the following projects in this book, we extend a special word of thanks:

- *Beaded Cross Stitch Ornaments*, page 31: Jane Chandler
- *Joyful Cross Stitch Ornaments,* page 54: Deborah Lambein

Thanks also go to the people who assisted in making and testing projects in this book: Ruth Ann Epperson, Elizabeth James, and Phyllis Lundy.